LIBERALIZING SERVICE TRADE

STRATEGIES FOR SUCCESS

T0347409

CHATHAM HOUSE PAPERS

General Series Editor: William Wallace
International Economics Programme Director: DeAnne Julius

Chatham House Papers are short monographs on current policy problems which have been commissioned by the Royal Institute of International Affairs. In preparing the paper, authors are advised by a study group of experts convened by the RIIA. Publication of the paper by the Institute indicates its standing as an authoritative contribution to the public debate.

The Royal Institute of International Affairs is an independent body which promotes the rigorous study of international questions and does not express opinions of its own. The opinions expressed in this publication are the responsibility of the author.

CHATHAM HOUSE PAPERS

LIBERALIZING SERVICE TRADE

STRATEGIES FOR SUCCESS

Phedon Nicolaides

The Royal Institute of International Affairs

Routledge
London

First published 1989
by Routledge
11 New Fetter Lane, London EC4P 4EE

Transferred to Digital Printing 2004

Reproduced from copy supplied by
Stephen Austin and Sons Ltd, Hertford,

British Library Cataloguing in Publication Data

Nicolaides, Phedon, 1958–
    Liberalizing service trade. – (Chatham House papers)
    1. Service industries
    I. Title II. Royal Institute of International Affairs
    III. Series
    338.4

    ISBN 0–415–04216–X

CONTENTS

For Ans and Alexander

ACKNOWLEDGMENTS

I have been greatly encouraged and assisted in the writing of this paper by DeAnne Julius, Director of the International Economics Programme at the Royal Institute of International Affairs, who has provided many insights and helpful suggestions. I am indebted to the members of the Study Group on Services, which met at Chatham House to discuss successive drafts. Although their comments have definitely shaped the paper, the opinions expressed here are my responsibility alone. My thanks also go to other colleagues at Chatham House who read and commented on various parts of the manuscript; to Michael Klein, Anna Merrick and Kathy Oswald, whose assistance in the preparation of the paper was much appreciated; and to the members of the Publications Department, who worked so hard to ensure the text's speedy publication.

January 1989   P.N.

The International Economics Programme

The project which gave rise to this paper forms part of the International Economics Programme of the Royal Institute of International Affairs. This programme seeks to provide clear analyses and practical policy recommendations for resolving international economic conflicts and strengthening the functioning of the world economy. It covers the economics and international politics of monetary, trade, finance, and investment issues.

Sponsors of the Programme include the American Express Bank, the Bank of England, the BOC Group, the Department of Trade and Industry, H.M. Treasury, Lloyds Bank, Merrill Lynch, Midland Bank, Morgan Grenfell, Royal International, RTZ, and S.G. Warburg.

1

THE CHALLENGE OF REFORMING POLICY ON SERVICES

Trade policy used to be about tariffs – whether to raise them or to lower them. In the nineteenth and early twentieth centuries, when government involvement in the economy was minimal, the purpose of the tariff was either to raise revenue or to further strategic and mercantilist objectives. Once economists were convinced that free trade was the optimum policy, it became relatively easy to prescribe the appropriate course of action. Governments were advised to reduce their tariffs and allow goods to be traded unobstructedly.

Trade policy today has little to do with tariffs. For one thing, most tariffs have been either reduced or bound as a result of successive rounds of multilateral trade negotiations under the auspices of the General Agreement on Tariffs and Trade (GATT). For another, governments have been ingenious in devising new policy measures for discriminating in favour of their own national firms. Their motives for intervention in the economy have also multiplied. Most unsettling for the old prescription of free trade, there are now many theoretically sound reasons why governments may have to intervene to restrict trade.

The process by which trade policy is determined in most western countries is much more complex today than it used to be only a few decades ago. Because governments have assumed a more active role in managing their own economies, they also have to monitor and assess the ever-increasing interaction among economies, especially because foreign and domestic public policies have a significant effect on trade. Not only is this interaction intensifying, but it is also

1

diversifying. Of course, international exchange has never been only about goods. Movement of capital and people has always been an essential part of entrepreneurial and colonial commerce. Since capital and people offer services, trade in services is not a new phenomenon. What makes it qualitatively new is the *way* in which it is taking place. Physical movement by capital or people is rapidly being displaced by other forms of trade. Technological progress is making possible the trade of services without those who provide them or those who consume them ever having to leave their countries. Technological advancement is also making possible the provision of new and more sophisticated services which were unavailable only a few years ago (e.g. simultaneous dealing of shares in different stock exchanges).

Many governments are now actively considering how to respond to the increasing amount and diversity of services that cross their borders. And they have to reconsider their policy on services because services are an essential component of any economic activity. Their importance has been obscured by the fact that the term 'services' comprises many, very diverse activities. Chapter 2 reviews the various meanings and definitions of the term and proposes a way of looking at services which can help in understanding the problems of liberalizing trade in services.

An aspect of services which has prompted governments to begin reconsidering their policy is the variety of ways by which services can be traded. Despite technological advancement, some services can be supplied only through personal contact between the client and the person who performs the service. Satellite television may provide you with entertainment from any place on earth but you still have to visit your barber or hairdresser. Movement of either the provider or the client may, therefore, be necessary. But, if the provider moves to another country, can this movement still be classified as trade or is it an act of foreign investment? Chapter 3 uses the definition proposed in Chapter 2 to examine the extent to which trade of services can be logically differentiated from investment. It is argued that there is no need to distinguish between the two if the purpose is to facilitate transactions in services between residents and foreigners. The mode of transaction should not be a cause for preventing that transaction from taking place.

Yet many governments obstruct such transactions on the grounds that foreigners offer services of allegedly lower quality than that expected from domestic providers. Trade is tightly controlled in the name of consumer protection. This objective does not necessarily mean that the invisible hand of the market should be amputated. But regulation to protect consumers is often used as a pretext to justify measures that reduce competition and exclude foreign firms from domestic markets. Chapter 4 examines how a distinction can be made between legitimate, or appropriate, regulations and discriminatory regulations that prevent foreign firms from operating in domestic markets. That chapter also defines, in broad terms, the 'zero-tariff equivalent' for services: i.e. the yardstick by which 'free' trade in services can be measured.

This paper concentrates primarily on restrictions on foreign service-providers, rather than on the appropriate level or strictness of regulation in a market, since its main objective is to examine how discriminatory policies against foreign providers can be identified and eliminated. Nevertheless, as explained in Chapter 4, elimination of trade barriers may also have to be accompanied by some relaxation of the strictness of regulatory control or some modification of the method by which regulation is administered. The invisible hand could work better if regulators were a little less visible.

The problem of distinguishing between appropriate and discriminatory regulation has been one of the chief difficulties encountered by countries which have been attempting to open up their trade either unilaterally or multilaterally. Chapter 5 reviews the experience of the European Community (EC) as it proceeds towards unification of its internal market by 1992. The Community's experience highlights the difficulty of removing trade impediments which are deeply embedded in a country's economic system and institutions. The EC was faced with two polar options. Either it could replace national regulations with Community regulations, or it could allow member countries to retain their own, and in many respects disparate, regulations. In the event, it has chosen a combination of these two opposites. The process of harmonizing all the diverse national rules would have been interminable and very acrimonious. On the other hand, liberalization without some harmonization would have resulted in 'competition among rules'. Each member country would have an incentive to adjust its own rules to attract footloose service industries by undercutting the rules of other countries.

3

The question which arises is whether the EC's approach of a mixture of harmonization and liberalization can be successfully replicated by other countries. Chapter 6, which examines the progress of the current GATT negotiations on services, suggests that GATT cannot realistically be expected to adopt the EC's model. GATT lacks the political cohesion and the institutions to implement that model effectively. Because it is unlikely that all GATT members will sign an agreement on services, it becomes imperative that an eventual agreement is prevented from degenerating into an exclusive club of a few countries. At the same time, however, a country would have an incentive to join that agreement only if it cannot derive the benefits while remaining outside it. Therefore, given that membership of the agreement is unlikely to be universal, the challenge for GATT is to encourage membership while preventing the agreement from becoming an exclusive club that undermines the multilateral foundation of the postwar trading system.

The treatment of non-members is not the only challenge. Another, already divisive, issue is the treatment of members who would demand special status. Many developing countries have opposed a GATT agreement on services. But, to the extent that they might concede to such an agreement, they have made it clear that they expect 'special and differential' treatment. Chapter 7 asks what form this special and differential treatment could take.

There is one major theme that runs throughout this paper: a liberal trade policy for services requires reliance on non-discriminatory rules. As elaborated in the following chapter, services are processes which in many respects are inseparable from those who provide them and their activities. Ultimately a policy that regulates the provision of services is a set of rules on 'who does what and how'. But safeguarding the quality of services does not necessarily imply exclusion of foreign providers. It is sufficient to require them to comply with the same rules that apply to domestic firms.

Because of the EC's 1992 initiative and the current GATT talks on services, there has been much reference to the meaning of reciprocity in services liberalization. The only kind of reciprocal concession that makes economic sense and provides for true and irreversible liberalization is an agreement to extend to foreign firms which operate in the domestic market the same treatment as that accorded to other domestic firms: i.e. non-discriminatory application of domestic regulations. The traditional liberalizing approach of reciprocally reducing particular trade restrictions cannot be applied as effectively in services as was applied in goods. The majority of goods are treated as other national goods as soon as they are allowed to cross a country's frontier. Since the concept of a frontier is not well defined in services, liberalization that proceeds on the basis of reciprocal concessions on particular policy measures implies that foreign service-providers would still be treated differently even after they cross a country's physical frontier. Removal of physical border barriers would not eliminate discrimination. As long as an element of discrimination remained in the system, governments would have an incentive to change the rules in favour of their national firms even after they agree to open up their markets to foreign competition. Liberalization will take hold only if governments commit themselves to the rule of equal treatment of all firms under their jurisdiction.

Of course, it may be argued that things cannot get worse than the existing state of rife discrimination and trade obstruction. Although this view is in some respects understandable, it fails to recognize the important element of expectation of 'fair play' in trade diplomacy. If for some reason the process of multilateral liberalization is reversed, bilateral games of one-upmanship will almost certainly fill the void. Those countries whose expectations of forthcoming benefits are disappointed because other countries do not honour their commitments would come under pressure by domestic groups to retaliate. A series of retaliatory and counter-retaliatory moves would severely dislocate and reduce world trade. There is more at stake in a failed bid to liberalize than in continuing with existing protectionism.

2
THE NATURE OF SERVICES

In order to be able to study services we must know what they are. They can be defined in two ways. The first method, which is ad hoc, simply groups together certain activities and calls them services. This method would be adequate if businessmen were to stop innovating. Once firms engage in new activities there is the question of where they can be classified. It becomes necessary to define criteria for distinguishing in a consistent manner what might be a service. Hence, the second method is systematic, defining services on the basis of certain criteria.

There is another reason why the ad-hoc method is not satisfactory. There can be many possible ways of grouping together different economic activities, not all of which are equally useful. A definition is useful if it helps towards better understanding of the effects, implications or consequences of what is being defined. The objective of this chapter is to define services in a systematic and useful way. For the purpose of this study, a useful way is one which helps us to understand how trade in services may be liberalized and how services may be regulated if need be.

The chapter reviews the various definitions of services that have been proposed and also examines how services are measured and classified in national accounting systems. There exists no precise method for measuring services. In consequence, the traditional approach to trade liberalization, which matches concessions of equivalent magnitude, is unlikely to be appropriate for services. Moreover, if, as suggested in this chapter, services are activities or processes, then a more suitable method of liberalization would involve the adoption of rules that apply to the operations of service-providers. The exchange of equivalent concessions would be more relevant for goods, which can be more easily identified.

Defining services

In a paradoxical way, the more intensively services are studied, the less certainty there is about how they can be defined and classified. According to Gershuny and Miles (1983), the term 'services' has four distinct uses. It may refer to industry (the firms that produce services), products (which are not exclusively produced by service firms), occupations (classification of labour markets) or functions (classification of activities). This chapter reviews the various definitions of the term services as used to describe particular functions or activities. Table 2.1 shows those economic activities which are classified as services in national accounting systems.

Most definitions attempt to convey the essence of services by identifying how they differ from goods, which, in this respect, provide a benchmark. By using goods as a benchmark of comparison, these definitions are systematic but, as argued below, they are not very useful because they do not explain what purpose they serve by perceiving services as something different from goods. Goods are defined as 'tangible', 'visible' and 'storable' or 'permanent'. Conversely, services are defined as 'intangible', 'invisible' and 'non-storable' or 'transient'. Goods can be exchanged, whereas services are produced by one economic agent for another and are consumed simultaneously with production. (For an exhaustive review of definitions of services, see Feketekuty, 1988.)

These features, however, cannot describe all of what are conventionally understood as services. For example, insurance is intangible and invisible but is not transient. A haircut is visible and does have some permanence, whereas a live musical performance is also visible but transient. Definitions which are based on the characteristics of intangibility and transience seem to obscure rather than clarify the meaning of services.

This problem arises partly because these definitions do not specify what the identified characteristics refer to. Do they refer to the production (i.e. performance) of a service or to its output (i.e. intended effects)? The act of performing a service may be temporary

Table 2.1 The Standard Industrial Classification (SIC)

SIC number	Service sector	SIC number	Service sector
40–49	Transportation, Communication, Utilities	75	Auto repair
		76	Miscellaneous repairs
50–51	Wholesale	78	Motion pictures
52–59	Retail	79, 84	Amusement, Recreation
60–67	Finance, Insurance, Real estate	80	Health
		81	Legal services
70	Hotels, Lodging places	82	Education
72	Personal services	83	Social services
73	Business services	91–97	Government

Source: Singelmann (1978).

but the effects need not be. For example, some professors claim that their lectures have lifelong effects on their students.

An adequate definition must, *inter alia*, make a distinction between the process of production and the product of a service. It must also clarify the meaning of 'transience'. Does it refer to a specific length of time? Is it a relative term, simply indicating that goods are more permanent than services? But how can it accommodate the fact that a lecture, or occasionally a bank transaction, is longer than the lifetime of an ice-cream? Or does it mean that production and consumption of services must take place at the same time? As argued later, not only is this 'simultaneity' requirement not applicable to many services (e.g. pension management, investment analysis) but it also depends on the way the intended output of a service is given to consumers (e.g. one may 'consume' a doctor's prescription at one's discretion).

In attempting to differentiate between the performance and effects of services, Hill (1977, p. 318) has defined a service as 'a change in the condition of a person, or of a good belonging to some economic unit, which is brought about as the result of the activity of some other economic unit, with prior agreement of the former person or economic unit'. A haircut is certainly a service. But how should insurance or investment advice be classified? When insurance brokers write a policy, the last thing they want is for the policy to induce a change in the condition or behaviour of the insured person. Is insurance a service only after a claim is filed? In the case of any kind of professional advice there need not be any automatic change in the condition of anybody. Professional consultation may actually result in no change, or may be intended to prevent change. The term 'change' requires clarification. By emphasizing 'change', which is the end-result or effect of a service, Hill's definition cannot really distinguish between services, goods and other effects of economic activities. The acquisition of a good does change somebody's endowment. Intuitively we know that a good is an object, whereas a service is a process. A definition of services, therefore, should focus on the process aspect of a service rather than its effect.

According to Riddle (1986), 'services are economic activities that provide time, place and form utility while bringing about a change in or for the recipient of the service. Services are produced by (a) the producer acting for the recipient; (b) the recipient providing part of the labour; and/or (c) the recipient and the producer creating the service in interaction'. Riddle's definition is more comprehensive than others. It accounts for the time element in the intended or expected effects of services. It also recognizes that many services are 'co-produced' by the provider and the client. A management consultant, for example, would hardly be able to provide a service unless he/she were guided with respect to the client's intentions, strengths and weaknesses. A lesson would hardly be worth having unless the student (or client) made an effort together with the instructor (or provider).

It is interesting to note how definitions of services have evolved. Early attempts sought to identify their physical peculiarities and the principal characteristics that distinguish them from goods. They were not very successful. Too many counter-examples and exceptions could be found. Later definitions, such as those by Hill and Riddle, have shifted their focus to the production of services, rather than their differences from goods, and have tended to look – usefully – at services as a particular kind of economic transaction.

Services as processes

By contrast to goods, which are objects, a service may be thought of as a process. A service can then be defined as an agreement or undertaking by the service-provider to perform now or in the future a series of tasks over a specified period of time towards a particular objective. The end-result (objective) of a service need not produce a change in the recipient's condition. There are several advantages in perceiving services as a transaction involving the execution of particular tasks.

First, it answers the question of whether services cause changes to consumers. The answer is that services do not necessarily have to result in a change and, if they do, the change may be contingent upon other events taking place. The important feature of a service is the agreement by the service-provider to act in a particular way should something else happen (e.g. insurance, honouring bank cheques).

Second, it allows the requirement for simultaneous and transient production and consumption to be dropped. For example, the management of pension contributions involves a long-term relationship between providers and clients, but, if the pension is provided as a lump-sum, there is no simultaneity between production and consumption, unless it can be claimed that people 'consume' contractual obligations.

Third, it avoids the logical difficulties of those definitions of services which identify only the intended change(s). It could be argued that consumers buy nothing else but goods or some other commodity which is specified in time and space. Why, for example, is the purchase of a meal in a restaurant called a service? Isn't it a purchase of different agricultural products which are delivered in a specified condition (cooked) at a particular place and time?

The problem of distinguishing between goods and services becomes even more difficult in the case of services which are 'embodied' in goods. Consider, for example, architectural and engineering design and computer-programming activities, which are customarily regarded as services. Isn't the ultimate purpose of a client the purchase of a drawing (a good) which depicts a design or the sequence of programming instructions? Moreover, is marketing consultancy, for example, a service only when the results are communicated orally and not submitted in a written report? It has been suggested that basic computer programmes could be classified as goods, and customized programmes could be classified as services. But why should customization qualify a programme to be a service, and where is the cut-off point? Taken to their logical extremes, these arguments would suggest that most services are an illusion, since consumers buy only goods which are specified by their physical, time-and-space attributes. A Marxist, however, would retort that everything can be reduced to its service components, since goods cannot be produced on their own and their value reflects the amount of 'embodied' labour.

A way to resolve this dilemma is to define a service as an explicit transaction involving the execution of, or the promise to execute, one or more specified tasks. Most people buy their cars fully assembled. In principle, one could buy all the individual components and then have them assembled. The end-result is exactly the same, yet the former is a good whereas the latter is a service. The crucial difference is the method and nature of the transaction by which the consumer acquires the car. The service transaction requires the execution of a series of tasks. To put it starkly, many services (e.g. financial services) are inseparable from the underlying contractual relationship between provider and consumer. This, in turn, implies that some services (e.g. the making of a portrait by Andy Warhol) are indistinguishable from the activities of their providers, and that they cannot therefore exist independently of their providers and their markets in the way that goods do. Hence, what is a service depends neither on some immutable natural law nor on the characteristics of the output or performance of a service. It depends on how economic agents transact and on which aspect of economic activity is examined. The greater the degree of specialization in an economy the greater the extent of services, if only because more transactions take place among economic agents.

There is an additional reason for perceiving services as a particular form of economic transaction. Services can be examined using standard tools of economic analysis. Within neoclassical economics, value is created by voluntary exchange. Thus, when a government intends to improve economic efficiency and welfare, it should aim at liberalizing transactions between service-providers and consumers. There has recently been much debate at GATT about what is a traded service and what constitutes a barrier to trade. It follows from the proposed definition of services that a barrier is whatever raises transaction costs artificially. Definitions of traded services are likely to be ineffective, misleading or protectionist as long as they ignore the different possible ways by which transactions may take place. It has been suggested, for example, that a traded service is one which involves no cross-border movement of the service-provider. This restricts the scope of traded services to a particular type of transaction, in which the output of a service can be embodied in a good or encoded in electronic signals so that there can be cross-border trade. Comprehensive liberalization would require elimination of all transaction barriers irrespective of where they occur.

The proposed definition also indicates the nature of the problem of measuring services. The problem is not in obtaining adequate data on expenditure but in knowing the nature of implicit or explicit contracts that economic agents enter into. Those who claim that liberalization of services cannot begin unless the full extent of trade is known are only partially correct. More statistics will improve our understanding of trade flows, but they can never provide the full picture. The following section examines how services are measured and classified in national accounting systems.

Measuring and classifying services
Statistics on services have two major defects. They are unsystematic and incomplete. They are unsystematic in that they do not measure services according to a methodology that serves any particular purpose. And they are incomplete because they do not measure every activity which may be classified as a service. Incompleteness may be reduced by more comprehensive reporting, but it can never be totally eliminated. There is more to be gained from trying to impart rationality to the various classification systems. For example, suggestions for making a clearer distinction between producer and consumer services could much improve trade statistics as well. The nature of trade statistics is examined more closely in Chapter 3.

In national accounting systems there are two primary ways of classifying services: (a) on the basis of production, whereby services are classified according to their origin or to which industry they are produced in; (b) on the basis of consumption, whereby services are classified according to the distribution of household expenditure.

Most OECD countries have adopted the production approach, on the basis of which they have developed the Standard Industrial Classification system (SIC) shown in Table 2.1. Yet different national systems are characterized more by their heterogeneity than by similarities. As Ochel and Wegner (1987, p. 13) note, different systems mix 'various activities with extremely different production characteristics and the residual sector "other services" . . . represents a large and growing share of total activities in most countries'.

In an attempt to improve upon existing systems, Browning and Singelmann (1975) have proposed the following scheme:

(a) distributive services (e.g. transport, communications, wholesale and retail trade, storage);
(b) business services (e.g. finance, insurance, accounting, advertising, R&D);
(c) social services (e.g. health, education, welfare); and
(d) personal services (e.g. hotels, restaurants, domestic services, repair).

Ochel and Wegner (1987, p. 14) observe that the advantage of the Browning-Singelmann proposal is that it relates services in terms of their economic functions. Its disadvantage is that it does not separate producer from consumer services, and in this sense it does not improve upon the SIC system. For example, transportation, finance and hotels provide services to both businesses and households.

The main difficulty in devising a classification system is that many services can be consumer or producer services depending on who buys them (e.g. postal services, banking, transportation). The difference that may arise is usually one of degree rather than of quality (e.g. catering, cleaning, communications). Even though qualitative differences can certainly be found (e.g. corporate hedging of exchange-rate risk vs sale of foreign currency to individuals), it is not clear where the dividing line lies.

The difficulty of measuring and classifying services is compounded by the fact that some services are an integral part of any productive or commercial activity (e.g. management, book-keeping). The size of such services could be measured only in an ideal economy in which extensive specialization prevails and everything has a market. National statistics will understate the size of these services as long as firms or individuals do some of their own book-keeping, marketing, repairing, etc.

In a sense, some services are an integral part of even the simplest of activities of any economic agent. Not only is it difficult to define precisely the boundaries of various services, since different activities blend into each other; it is also difficult to obtain an accurate measure of services, since no one accounts exactly for what he or she is doing at any point in time. As long as services are perceived to be a series of tasks, it may be impossible to gain a complete picture of the

size of services in an economy. It may also be theoretically impossible to define what the complete picture should look like.

Services are generally reported in terms of value. Detailed classification would require a definition of the output of different services.
Baumol (1985) argues that in principle service output is not more
difficult to measure than goods. This may be correct for services such
as hairdressing (number of haircuts) or transportation (number of
trips or passengers). But what is the output of banking? Is it the
number of customers, the value of transactions (which transactions?) or the size of the assets? There is also the problem of whether
output or input should be measured. Should education, for example,
be measured in terms of number of pupils, number of teachers or
hours of teaching? The growth of communication and information
technologies (i.e. the packaging, bundling of services) blurs the
boundaries among services, increases their complexity and impairs
even more their measurement.

Petit (1986) reports that in the national accounts of the USA, 36%
of real gross product originating in the total service industry is
estimated by using labour proxies, and 48% by using profit-margin
indicators. Thus more than 80% of the production of services is
measured by proxies. A common defect of national accounting
systems is that they ignore quality differences, technological
improvements and productivity gains. Service proxies are even less
capable of conveying information on the magnitude of such
changes. Smith (1972) has found that service output is systematically
and significantly underestimated by employment proxies. The same
proxies impart an upward bias to service prices because a greater
proportion of change in prices is attributed to inflation than to
quality or productivity gains.

Finally, a substantial source of mismeasurement is the leakage
caused by the black economy. It is widely believed that the size of
unreported activities is much greater for services than for goods (see,
e.g., Blades, 1982). It is easier to hide intangible output.

Such are some of the difficulties in measuring and classifying
services. Indeed, there seems to be no ideal system. Any system is
bound to be incomplete and, therefore, to leave some vagueness and
arbitrariness at the boundaries of the different service sectors.
Nevertheless, there is room for improvement. The prevailing
opinion among experts is that there could be a clearer distinction
between producer and consumer services, so that there can be a

better understanding of the extent to which services are used as inputs into other activities. However, improvement in national statistics would not necessarily improve trade statistics. The special problems of balance-of-payments statistics are examined in the next chapter.

Defining services in GATT

At every GATT round there is a conflict between the 'pragmatists' and the 'purists'. The pragmatists are those that identify specific policy measures to be put on the agenda with the consent of the negotiating parties. The purists want to define general terms or principles so that everything falling within their purview is automatically on the agenda without requiring the consent of the negotiators. In other words, the purists want to define the rules of selecting the items of the agenda.

This conflict is part of a recurring difficulty encountered at every round. Each round involves two-level negotiations. Initially there is bargaining to determine the shape of the agenda; afterwards there is bargaining about the items already on the agenda. Every GATT negotiator knows that bargaining power depends on the size and nature of exchanged concessions, which in turn depend on the items under negotiation.

Even though more than two years have passed since the launching of the Uruguay round, delegates have not been able to agree on a definition of services and especially that of traded services. Developing countries favour a narrow definition, because they think they stand to 'lose', whereas developed countries insist on a wider definition, because they think they are likely to 'gain'. The question which needs to be answered here is whether it is necessary to have a definition of services before negotiators proceed to more substantial issues. Moreover, is it possible to have a precise definition, and what are the consequences of adopting it? And should there be a distinction between definitions and the service sectors covered by the negotiations? Determining coverage is essentially a bargaining problem. For the reasons explained below, deciding on a definition is a more complex problem with serious repercussions.

Those who want a definition are motivated by the traditional GATT approach to liberalization. Concessions are granted in such a way as to balance benefits and costs, which are usually measured in terms of gained or lost market share or trade volume. In previous rounds, balance was sought by defining the nature and magnitude of the reduction in duties on specified products. There was no attempt to derive a general definition of goods. So what is the purpose of seeking a general definition of services? Is it that it could facilitate the subsequent definition of those services that could be subject to negotiation? But is it possible to define precisely particular services or service products? A precise definition should be capable of distinguishing one service from another.

As long as the negotiations are confined to services embodied in goods, the same precision is theoretically feasible. The following chapter considers the issues that arise out of the distinction between traded (e.g. embodied in goods) and non-traded services. Should the scope of the negotiations be extended to measures that exclude foreign providers from national markets, it would be difficult to predict the nature of transactions that would take place once foreign providers were allowed to operate in the internal market. Consequently, it would also be difficult to establish the size of potential gains and losses and achieve a balance of concessions. Knowing the effects of liberalization would require the imposition of extensive regulations defining the extent and nature of permissible activities by foreign service-providers. Attempting a precise definition of services will result in the creation of further trade restrictions. Either the activities of foreign providers will be restricted to fit exactly the boundaries of the definition, or governments will feel free to implement new discriminatory policies that fall outside those boundaries.

Negotiators should also consider whether an exact definition is possible even in principle. Precise definitions are certain to be very narrow, fraught with exceptions and special cases. It is not easy to define the essence of activities comprising tasks that may be executed in many different combinations. The view that a definition is necessary reflects experience gained from liberalizing trade in goods. Since services are processes, there could be many possible ways of achieving the objective or result desired by a client. Identifying the outcome of a service does not necessarily mean that the restrictions on the operations of service-providers will be negotiated away or that others will not replace them. Liberalization will be more likely to be of real substance if negotiators start identifying the impediments to transactions between domestic consumers and foreign providers. The fact that precise measures of services are non-existent also implies that the exchange of equivalent concessions, as in the case of goods, is neither meaningful nor likely to be successful. When each country has a plethora of distinct policies, the matching of equivalent policies of equivalent effect is certainly not an easy task. To eliminate discrimination in the provision of services, both domestic and foreign service-providers need to be subject to the same rules. Since services are processes, negotiators should examine the effect and importance of rules, especially because many services are heavily regulated. Exact definitions are an elusive goal and they cannot serve the purpose for which negotiators have been demanding them without resulting in further trade barriers.

3
PRODUCTION AND TRADE OF SERVICES

The production, consumption and trade of those activities classified as services are continually increasing in both developed and developing countries. Services contribute now more than half of the total output of western economies. As a result, governments are being forced to reconsider their policies towards services. They have realized that existing policies are either inappropriate or incapable of coping with the expansion of services in terms of volume and sophistication.

Some of them are also beginning to realize that obsolete policies are a handicap to industries striving to survive in an ever more competitive world. This chapter argues that before policy-makers determine their countries' trade policies, they should consider the peculiarities of services and the reasons for which they have grown. It does not attempt to present a model for a proper policy on services; rather, it identifies some important characteristics of services which must be taken into account in the process of determining trade policy.

This chapter also examines the concept of trade in services, how trade is measured and which countries trade in which services. It is shown that no country is completely self-sufficient in services, which suggests that there is scope for beneficial specialization through liberalization. However, it will be difficult to achieve liberalization through a process of exchanging concessions of equivalent magnitude or yielding equivalent benefits. The poor quality of the data, which are highly aggregated and incomplete, prevents any meaningful comparison of concessions. GATT negotiators and trade officials have so far shown little understanding of the true complexity of some of the proposals for liberalization on the basis of equivalent concessions.

The changing economy
The rising interest in services is not unjustified. In 1960, industrial countries generated 40% of their GDP in manufacturing and 54% in services; in 1986, manufacturing contributed 36% and services 61%. For developing countries, in 1960 agriculture accounted for 34% of their GDP and services 40%; in 1986, agriculture contributed 18% and services 48%. Services also provide more than half of the overall employment in industrial countries. Among industrial countries, the United States and the United Kingdom have the largest share of service-generated employment, with 71% and 66%, respectively.

Services have overtaken the production of goods as the major source of value-added in western economies. Table 3.1 shows the share of goods and services in total value-added (measured at factor cost) for the OECD countries during 1980–84. If construction is excluded from services, then the mean OECD share of value-added for goods is 42% and 57% for services. If construction is included in services, their share rises to 64% and that of goods declines to 36%. Even if 'non-market' services are subtracted, the remaining 'market' services add more value than agriculture, mining and manufacturing put together. The only exception is Turkey, whose agriculture is still the second largest sector in the economy, contributing 20% of total value-added.

The real value-added of services has grown faster than that of goods. The growth rates shown in Table 3.2 are calculated as GDP elasticities. They are derived by dividing the growth rates for real value-added by the growth rate of total GDP. There are two reasons for expressing them as GDP elasticities. It is safer to make comparisons between countries which have had different growth rates. It also offsets some of the effect of cyclical fluctuations caused by the expansion of the 1960s and the stagnation of the 1970s. As can be seen in Table 3.2, the growth of real value-added in finance, real estate and business services has been higher than in any other major activity. It is worth noting the exceptionally high growth in financial services experienced by the UK and Luxembourg. The UK is the

Table 3.1 Goods and services in total value-added, 1980–84 average (%)

Country	GOODS			SERVICES						
					Market services			Non-market services		
	Total	Manufacturing	Construction	Total	Wholesale, retail	Transport & communications	Finance, real estate	Community, social	Government	Private non-profit
Canada	38	19	6	62	—	8	13	—	17	2
US	35	22	4	65	17	6	21	8	13	—
Japan	43	28	8	57	—	6	14	—	8	2
Australia	39	16	6	—	—	7	21	—	8	—
New Zealand	41	23	5	59	21	8	14	3	12	1
Austria	44	29	8	56	17	6	14	3	14	1
Belgium	36	23	6	64	—	8	13	—	14	1
Denmark	34	19	6	66	14	8	16	5	23	2
Finland	46	26	8	54	11	8	14	4	15	1
France	41	27	7	59	13	6	18	9	13	2
W. Germany	45	33	6	55	11	8	—	—	12	1
Greece	48	19	7	52	13	6	—	—	10	2
Italy	46	28	8	54	15	6	12	14	13	1
Luxembourg	39	27	7	61	16	5	15	12	12	1
Netherlands	39	18	7	61	13	6	12	5	14	1
Norway	46	15	7	54	14	10	8	—	14	—
Portugal	48	28	7	53	21	5	9	10	11	1
Spain	47	26	8	53	17	7	13	4	9	1
Sweden	39	24	8	61	12	7	7	6	25	1
Turkey	53	24	4	47	16	10	7	6	8	—
UK	42	24	6	58	12	7	18	5	15	1
Mean	43	24	7	57	15	7	14	7	14	1

Source: Blades (1986).

Table 3.2 Growth rates of real value-added, 1960–83 (%)

Country	GOODS			SERVICES						
				Market services				Non-market services		
	Total	Manufac- turing	Con- struction	Total	Wholesale, retail	Transport & communications	Finance, real estate	Community, social	Government	Private non-profit
Canada	0.81	0.96	0.62	1.06	—	1.29	1.29	—	0.79	0.80
US	0.81	1.01	0.13	1.13	1.16	1.29	1.49	1.06	0.68	—
Japan	1.10	1.56	0.43	0.98	—	1.03	1.06	—	0.61	1.26
Australia	0.65	0.25	0.07	—	—	1.74	1.35	—	—	-0.96
New Zealand	1.24	1.32	-1.16	0.75	0.00	1.71	1.55	1.24	0.82	-0.02
Austria	0.95	1.07	0.94	1.06	1.11	1.32	1.55	0.97	0.79	-0.15
Belgium	0.94	1.19	1.00	1.06	—	0.74	1.20	1.11	1.23	-0.96
Denmark	0.72	1.18	-0.52	1.29	0.83	0.40	1.72	0.64	2.08	0.19
Finland	0.85	1.26	0.62	1.11	1.05	1.10	1.35	0.90	1.20	0.27
France	0.98	0.95	0.82	1.08	0.93	1.22	1.39	1.10	0.63	0.50
W. Germany	0.88	1.01	0.50	1.17	0.91	1.30	—	—	1.09	—
Greece	0.94	1.27	0.54	1.09	—	1.36	1.09	—	0.92	0.32
Italy	0.95	1.12	-0.09	1.01	1.24	1.24	—	—	0.68	1.29
Luxembourg	0.35	0.48	0.78	2.63	2.15	1.88	6.12	1.69	1.19	—
Norway	1.15	0.60	0.86	0.93	0.61	0.85	0.93	0.85	1.39	-0.82
Portugal	0.94	1.25	0.97	1.16	0.98	1.20	1.07	—	1.89	-0.08
Spain	1.01	1.40	0.85	0.98	0.89	1.61	—	—	0.96	-0.44
Sweden	0.65	0.61	0.35	1.13	0.81	2.00	0.96	1.35	1.44	—
Turkey	0.91	1.48	1.02	1.19	—	1.25	0.98	—	1.11	—
UK	1.04	-1.00	-1.23	0.96	-0.12	0.55	2.32	1.95	0.61	—
Mean	0.89	24	7	1.15	0.90	1.25	1.60	7	1.06	0.09

Source: Blades (1986).

21

only industrial country whose manufacturing sector actually declined during the 1960–83 period.

The faster growth of service activities has contributed to faster growth of employment in services. Table 3.3 shows that services contribute more than goods to overall employment. Even if the government sector is excluded, services still provide more employment than agriculture, mining and manufacturing. The share of services in total employment is bigger because employment opportunities have expanded faster than in goods. As shown in Table 3.4, the growth rate of employment in services has been higher than in goods over the past three decades. These growth rates are also calculated as employment elasticities. The growth rate of each sector is divided by the growth rate of overall employment. Statistics on services are imperfect. Nevertheless, the available information indicates that the activities which have been classified as services have been expanding. Why, one inevitably asks, has this pronounced structural shift taken place?

Some explanations

One answer is that the perceived rising importance of services is a statistical illusion. National statistical agencies are becoming more efficient in collecting service data; there are also more data to collect as more firms contract out previously in-house functions (i.e. the externalization hypothesis). This answer is unsatisfactory. Statistical illusion is probably a contributory factor, but it cannot explain why firms are contracting out an increasing proportion of their activities. Something else must be changing in the economy. The rising importance of services is not an isolated event. It is an integral part of a more general economic transformation. This phenomenon has been examined by, among others, Stanback (1979), Stanback et al. (1981), Inman (1985), Riddle (1986) and Giarini (1987).

The explanations which have been proposed look at changes in technology and market structure. Advances in technology, especially information technology, have enabled firms to automate their production processes and increase the sophistication (i.e. technological content) and 'customization' of their products so as better to serve the needs of their customers. In order to implement automation and customization, firms have had to train their staff, hire more educated personnel, improve their R&D departments and adjust

Table 3.3 Shares of goods and services in total employment, 1980–84 average (%)

Country	GOODS			SERVICES						
				Market services				Non-market services		
	Total	Manufac-turing	Con-struction	Total	Wholesale, retail	Transport & communications	Finance, real estate	Community, social	Government	Private non-profit
US	30	19	5	70	23	4	11	15	17	—
Japan	47	24	10	53	18	5	4	17	7	2
Australia	35	19	7	65	20	8	9	23	5	—
Belgium	35	23	7	65	19	7	—	5	19	3
Denmark	36	20	8	64	13	7	8	5	30	1
Finland	46	24	8	54	14	7	6	4	19	4
France	41	23	8	59	16	6	7	11	19	3
W. Germany	48	33	10	51	16	6	3	8	15	3
Iceland	47	24	8	53	13	7	6	7	17	2
Italy	47	26	8	52	20	6	—	—	15	2
Luxembourg	42	26	10	58	—	7	5	16	11	1
Netherlands	35	20	8	66	18	7	8	8	16	—
Norway	39	21	8	61	15	10	5	15	23	3
Portugal	54	20	10	45	12	4	2	6	9	1
Sweden	35	20	7	65	14	7	5	6	32	—
UK	37	—	6	64	—	6	—	—	22	—
Mean	41	23	8	57	17	7	6	11	17	2

Source: Blades (1986).

23

Table 3.4 Growth rates of employment, 1960–84 (%)

| Country | GOODS | | | SERVICES | | | | | | |
| | | | | Market services | | | | Non-market services | | |
	Total	Manufacturing	Construction	Total	Wholesale, retail	Transport & communications	Finance, real estate	Community, social	Government	Private non-profit
US	0.79	0.74	0.98	1.11	1.14	0.92	1.57	1.16	0.91	—
Japan	0.77	0.91	1.15	1.22	—	0.97	1.41	—	1.14	1.55
Australia	—	0.70	0.83	—	—	—	1.35	—	—	—
Belgium	0.71	0.72	0.69	1.25	1.05	1.00	—	0.96	1.42	0.78
Denmark	0.68	0.77	0.69	1.32	0.83	1.17	1.88	1.55	2.30	0.34
Finland	0.70	1.20	0.83	1.43	1.27	1.11	2.51	1.56	2.57	0.64
France	0.78	0.86	0.77	1.23	1.09	1.02	1.48	—	—	—
W. Germany	0.77	0.87	0.92	1.38	1.09	0.82	—	0.96	1.98	1.15
Iceland	0.87	1.01	0.95	1.15	1.03	1.51	1.46	—	1.37	2.44
Italy	0.69	—	0.88	1.56	1.45	1.03	—	—	1.82	0.96
Luxembourg	0.77	0.78	1.00	1.26	—	1.07	—	1.50	1.18	1.35
Netherlands	0.74	0.73	0.70	1.22	0.98	0.84	1.50	1.24	1.33	0.68
Norway	0.70	0.81	0.96	1.32	1.11	1.06	2.28	0.94	1.84	—
Sweden	0.74	0.78	0.70	1.22	0.93	0.94	1.30	—	1.60	0.67
UK	0.74	—	0.95	1.22	—	—	—	—	1.21	—
Mean	0.75	0.84	0.87	1.28	1.09	1.04	1.67	1.23	1.59	1.06

Source: Blades (1986).

Figure 3.1 The evolving economy

Old economy	New economy
(a) Standardized output Assembly lines	(a) Customized goods and services Increased variety and bundling of goods and services
(b) In-house production of services	(b) Externalization of services, networking, interlinkages
(c) Local, national markets	(c) Internationalization of production and competition
(d) Vertical integration Large corporations	(d) Vertical disintegration Small firms, large transnational conglomerates
(e) Rigid embodiment of technology	(e) Flexible production modes
(f) Material inputs, outputs	(f) Immaterial investments, human resource and knowledge-based inputs
(g) Factory, blue-collar employment	(g) Office, white-collar employment
(h) Sectoral regulation	(h) New forms of regulation

Source: Ochel and Wegner (1987).

their management methods and organizational structure. In the process, they have had to shed unnecessary or secondary activities not suited to their new structure.

New technology has been becoming available together with changes in market conditions. The rise in disposable income has enabled consumers to spend more on income-elastic services. The increase in demand for services has given an impetus to the establishment of firms specializing exclusively in the provision of services. This specialization, and the subsequent reaping of economies of scale, has provided an additional incentive for further contracting-out and expansion of the market for services. Instances of trade liberalization and improvement of international communications and transportation have also contributed to national specialization and to the expansion of national markets.

Ochel and Wegner (1987) provide a useful taxonomy of the salient features of what they call the 'old' and the 'new' economy. Figure 3.1 shows their taxonomy. The 'new', service-intensive economy has the following predominant characteristics:

(*a*) *Flexible production.* Computerized production technology (informatics, robotics) and the use of a more educated labour force introduce flexibility into the process of production. As a result, products can be varied to suit the requirements of different clients. The abandonment of conveyor-belt processes would not have been possible without the use of skilled workers, who could respond to the different demands of customized or variable production. Management had to decentralize so that the different units of a firm could become more responsive and show greater initiative in solving problems arising from the non-standardization of the production process.

(*b*) *Product transformation.* Not only have products become more differentiated with higher technological content; they are also increasingly provided in the form of bundles or packages of different functions. They can frequently be combined with other products or services. Especially in services, there is a tendency towards 'networking'. Networks allow many users to gain simultaneous access to an ever greater number of distinct services. For example, the expansion and improvement in telecommunication technology have made available services such as home banking and home shopping which may both use the same network. The expansion of networks has created economies of scale. The addition of new services to existing networks has created economies of scope whereby the cost of providing a service is reduced by the provision of further services.

(*c*) *Market transformation.* The shift towards flexible production, product bundles and networks has affected market structure in distinct ways. The minimum efficient scale of production has been reduced by the use of informatics and robotics. For example, in a newspaper a single person using a computer terminal can now function as a reporter, an editor and a typesetter. This has lowered barriers to entry for potential competitors. By contrast, the higher technological content of many products requires an ever greater amount of resources to be expended on research and development, thus raising entry barriers. The bundling of different products has also raised barriers to potential competitors. New firms can compete more effectively by offering a range of products. While each individual product can be efficiently manufactured at a lower scale, the development of new products and their marketing have created a tendency towards concentration of production and centralization of distribution.

(*d*) *Internationalization of the economy*. Internationalization has taken several forms. First, improvements in telecommunications and transportation have reduced the transaction costs of international exchange. Second, they have also reduced the effectiveness of trade barriers and national policies because trade may occur in different forms. For example, restrictions on the sale of engineering designs by foreigners may be circumvented by electronic transmission of a computerized version. Third, there has been a tendency towards globalization of corporate activity. Global companies locate their different departments or divisions in those countries in which they can derive maximum benefits from the special advantages or assets of each location. And, fourth, networks compete by linking more countries and more users and by offering a greater number of services. As in the case of national market structures, the internationalization of economies has created two opposing forces. There is pressure for both greater concentration and greater decentralization as new technology enables more firms to compete in international markets.

These explanations of the growth of services allow one to draw several conclusions regarding trade policy. First, some services are new economic activities, made possible by technological progress (e.g. mobile telecommunications). Hence, imports of such services are not likely to undermine directly any existing industries in countries which lack the necessary technology.

Second, many services (i.e. producer services) are used as inputs into other production processes. Without them production itself would have been impossible. Again, the countries that lack such services, or have lower-quality services, are likely not to be as competitive as other exporters of similar products. In a recent study, Tucker and Sundberg (1986) have found that Australian manufacturing exports have the highest amount of 'embodied' intermediate services among ASEAN countries. Countries with more developed service industries can presumably use more of those services to improve the quality of their manufacturing products.

Third, the knowledge and skills which are necessary for the provision of services are embodied in their providers (e.g. scientists, managers, lawyers, economists). These skills are acquired through long-term education or through training and experience gained 'on the job'. If most of these skills can be transferred by personal contact, a more flexible policy towards foreign service-providers may be necessary.

Fourth, participation in international markets requires access to international networks such as those which facilitate payments through interbank transfers. Such networks can be operated more efficiently only by a few companies in a few countries. Nevertheless, for a small country that cannot establish a rival network, having competitive exports also implies being able to use these networks and their services.

These arguments do not prove that the appropriate trade policy for services is that of free trade. For example, regulatory supervision, which is examined in Chapter 4, may require the imposition of trade restrictions. What they do suggest is that policy-makers have to consider the reasons for which services have been growing, and to appreciate the significance of the various peculiarities of services. One such feature, which has a particular bearing on trade policy, is the need for proximity between providers and consumers. The following section examines the concept of trade in services and its relation to movements of service-providers. If trade is to be facilitated, there must be an understanding of the different ways international transactions may take place. The section also examines how trade in services is measured and how movement of providers affects trade statistics.

Trade in services
Trade in goods is easy to define. It is the sale of merchandise or other commodities from one country to another. Trade occurs when the transfer of the property right of a good results in the physical crossing of national frontiers by that good. Nothing else is required. Hence, crossing of frontiers is both a necessary and a sufficient condition for trade to occur. Transactions in services are more varied. Whether trade in services entails cross-border movement depends on how narrowly the term 'transaction' is defined.

Services are transacted in several ways. They may require one or more of the following: (a) movement of providers to consumers; (b) movement of consumers to providers; (c) movement of both consumers and providers; and (d) no movement by either providers or consumers. These four categories are more extensively analysed by Bhagwati (1984), Hindley (1986b), Sampson and Snape (1985), Grubel (1986) and Feketekuty (1988).

No movement is necessary whenever the end-result or output of a service can either be embodied in a good which can then be traded separately, or be encoded and transmitted by electronic or other means. Such services are usually called 'traded' services. Services which are possible only when their providers or consumers move are called 'factor' or 'non-traded' services. By convention the movement of goods is regarded as trade, while the movement of factors of production (e.g. providers of services) is classified as investment. This distinction has motivated demands by developing countries that the current GATT negotiations on services should be limited to trade rather than investment issues. It has also been suggested that factor movement could be considered only if it is temporary, or if it simply 'supplies' a service without 'producing' it in the foreign market. Thus there are conflicting interpretations of what constitutes trade in services, especially since most developed countries want to include factor movement in the concept of trade. What are the implications of attempting to separate traded from non-traded services?

First consider the basic features of trade of goods. Transactions in goods require the transfer of property rights. It is not necessary that sellers or buyers move across a frontier as long as transportation (a service) is provided by a third party. In principle, therefore, transactions are facilitated by the removal of impediments to the movement of goods. Transactions in services cannot always be effected without a movement of the provider (e.g. transportation) or the consumer. Thus, for the purpose of facilitating or liberalizing *transactions* in services, it may also be necessary to remove barriers to the movement of people. The attempt to distinguish between traded and non-traded services is equivalent to claiming that there is a class of transactions which will not be liberalized. In the case of goods, investment is an alternative to trade. For many services, trade and investment are not substitutes. A narrow definition of trade is tantamount to preserving barriers to transactions in services.

Moreover, the meaning of the term 'traded services' is not as clear as it may seem at first glance. Some services are tradable because their output can be embodied in a good. Does this mean, for example, that even though a consultant is not able to open an office in a foreign country, he would be able to visit his client, write his report and send it by post? If the visit is considered to be part of the production process, would the client be allowed instead to send him all the relevant information so that the consultant would not have to make the visit? Would a company be allowed to send its books to foreign auditors? The reason these questions arise is that services are often wrongly perceived in terms of their output instead of as a process of particular tasks or activities. The distinction between traded and non-traded services is based, not on any economic principle, but on what is allowed by the prevailing technological capability to be embodied in goods. The objective of the GATT negotiations should be the liberalization of service activities irrespective of whether they fall within preconceived notions about the concept of trade.

It will be suggested later that the major barriers to transactions in services are restrictions on the activities by foreign service-providers and on the use of their services by domestic residents. In almost every country, people are prevented by legal constraints from buying insurance from abroad, even though the cross-border movement of pieces of paper (i.e. the insurance document) is free. Liberalizing the trade of services embodied in goods will not have any significant effect unless other domestic legal restrictions on the use of foreign-provided services are also removed. But if such restrictions are finally removed, what does it matter if services are provided via a good or through personal contact? If there is a difference, it is probably because absence of personal contact is an impediment which discriminates against foreign providers.

Available technology may allow a service to be provided without prior personal contact (e.g. opening a foreign bank account). It may therefore be argued that, for those services whose trade is technologically feasible, restrictions on the movement of providers should be permissible. Again, this view ignores the real issue, which is the removal of barriers to transactions. Even if there are no other discriminatory measures against foreign service-providers, domestic consumers may prefer to have personal contact with the providers. Restrictions on cross-border movement would prevent transactions from being carried out in *the most efficient way as determined by the market*. Since services may be transacted in different ways, the *effective* impediments to trade are those which raise the costs of the most efficient and least costly method of transaction. According to this line of reasoning, a barrier to trade or a discriminatory measure is also the requirement for movement of providers whenever such movement is unnecessary or not demanded by the market. Hence, what is an effective barrier in services depends on how the market requires services to be transacted. If the purpose of defining trade in services is to facilitate transactions, then a broad definition is in order.

A deficiency of trade statistics is that they do not fully account for the fact that services may also be traded by providers who move across borders. This is another reason why GATT negotiators will not get much help from trade statistics when attempting to agree on equivalent concessions. In addition to being imprecise and highly aggregated, statistics do not necessarily convey information on service firms that operate within national markets. The following section examines available trade statistics and the reasons for which they may be unsuitable as a basis for measuring equivalent liberalizing concessions.

Balance-of-payments data
The main source of statistical information on international transactions in services is the *Balance of Payments Yearbook* published by the IMF. Its coverage of the different service sectors varies according to the degree of detail provided by reporting countries. Most countries collect and report statistics on the following services: shipment, other transportation, passenger services, travel, other private and government services, investment income and unrequited transfers. For a few industrial countries there are more detailed entries, identifying transactions in communications, construction, engineering and insurance.

Balance-of-payments data suffer from all the statistical defects that were discussed in Chapter 2. They are not classified according to a methodology that is suited to services. They give even less information on the share of producer and consumer services in international transactions. Income arising from movement of providers may be classified in several categories, not all of which indicate that trade in services could have occurred.

The main source of mismeasurement of services is that many services are exported 'embodied' in goods. Tucker and Sundberg (1986), using input-output tables, have estimated that over a third of the value of Australia's manufacturing exports is attributed to embodied services. The recent anti-dumping dispute between the EC and Japan illustrates this point very well. Japanese manufacturers of photocopiers have established so-called 'screwdriver' plants in the Community, presumably to avoid anti-dumping charges. The Commission contends that these plants merely assemble components without doing adequate manufacturing in terms of adding value. Some of the plants are in Britain. Irrespective of whether these products have been dumped, Britain has been providing services to somebody. It is unknown where these services have been classified. Should they have been classified as exports of assembling services to Japan, or to France, Germany and other EC members? It is almost certain that they have not been counted as part of the invisibles in Britain's current account.

The 'invisibles' component of the current account comprises traded services, investment income and unrequited transfers. Traded or non-factor services include shipment, other transportation, passenger services, travel, other private services and other government services. The item 'other private services' includes labour income, property income and other services such as non-merchandise insurance, communications, advertising, brokerage, management, operational leasing or other charters, periodicals bought through subscription, processing and repair, merchanting and other professional and technical services. Unrequited transfers include migrants' transfers, workers' remittances and other official transfers.

Service data suffer from the same problems as other balance-of-payments statistics. First, they are not pure, in that they include expenditure on goods. The degree of impurity is unknown and may vary in different years or among different countries. Second, they cannot provide a comprehensive coverage of all service transactions, either because they are classified in other categories or because they are excluded completely. They are also highly aggregated, giving only a sum figure for several service sectors. Third, the classification of various service transactions is a matter of convention and is not based on economic principles. An example is the distinction between non-factor services and unrequited transfers, which is based on the definition of residency.

The pattern of trade in services
Given the preoccupation of trade officials with equivalent concessions, one can almost understand why most GATT member countries have been unenthusiastic about the prospect of liberalizing

Table 3.5 Invisible trade as a percentage of GNP

Country	Receipts		Payments	
	1972	1985	1972	1985
USA	2.1	3.1	1.3	2.2
Canada	3.6	4.3	6.5	9.2
UK	11.1	21.4	8.8	18.2
Austria	13.1	18.3	6.3	12.8
Belgium	10.8	37.9	9.4	35.3
France	4.5	11.1	4.1	9.5
Germany	3.5	6.1*	5.7	8.1
Italy	6.4	7.6	4.6	6.9*
Holland	14.7	20.2	11.1	12.2
Norway	19.3	15.1	12.8	18.9
Europe Total	6.9	12.3*	6.1	11.6
Other Developed	1.9	3.1*	3.5	4.5
— Japan	1.6	3.1	2.7	3.7
— Australia	2.6	2.9	6.3	7.9
Latin America	2.9	3.5*	5.6	8.4*
— Brazil	1.1	1.2*	4.6	5.9*
— Mexico	4.7	4.6	4.8	9.1
Asia	2.3	5.7*	3.5	7.6*
Africa	3.3	2.4*	9.8	8.3*
TOTAL	3.8	5.8*	3.8	6.3*

Source: BIEC (1987). Asterisks denote 1984 figures.

services. They look at the balance of invisible trade, and they see a few countries running persistent surpluses while most of the rest experience large and seemingly permanent deficits. Normally, this observation would be a strong enough inducement for liberalization because it would enable them to buy services from sources which are apparently more efficient than their own. But the logic of trade negotiations dictates otherwise.

Aggregated figures, however, belie the degree of diversity of individual country positions in different service industries. Neither have the exporting countries surpluses in all services, nor have the importing countries deficits in every service sector. Moreover, Germany and Japan, which have the largest export surpluses in manufacturing goods, also happen to have two of the largest deficits in invisibles. In 1985, Germany's deficit was $12.1 billion, almost as much as that of the whole of Africa. Japan's deficit was $8.5 billion. Canada had the largest deficit, running at $16.3 billion.

These deficits are not small in relation to the size of each country's GNP. Table 3.5 shows the invisible receipts and payments of selected countries as a percentage of their GNP. There are several European countries (e.g. Belgium, Holland, the UK) whose payments for imports of services represent a much larger proportion of their GNP than is the case for the average of Latin American, Asian and African countries. Hence, it is not true that industrial countries do not feel the 'burden' of large service imports. It is also worth noting that the low figure for the US is probably due to the fact that trade in general is relatively small in proportion to its GNP. Moreover, the figure for Latin America is likely to be exaggerated by debt-related payments.

Sectoral statistics reveal even greater diversity among different countries. Table 3.6 shows the receipts and payments of the five major industrial countries in individual service sectors. These countries do not run persistent surpluses in all services; they actually experience deficits in more than half of those sectors. Aggregate receipts may exceed aggregate payments, but such aggregate figures hide the substantial two-way flow of trade.

Among developing countries, which as a whole have a deficit in invisibles, there are quite a few which have surpluses in individual sectors such as shipping and travel. The largest source of earnings is the remittances of workers shown by unrequited transfers. Egypt, India and Pakistan each receive almost SDR 3 billion from their workers abroad. This amount is far greater than that of any industrial country, and it shows in which kind of services developing countries have a strong advantage.

There is a large literature in economics in favour of liberal trade because resources are utilized more efficiently and also because export potential improves (see Bhagwati, 1987 and Feketekuty, 1988). Hindley (1988a) and Hindley and Smith (1984) apply the former argument to services, and Balasubramanyam (1988a) uses the latter to suggest that the balance of trade of developing countries need not worsen as a result of liberalization. Indeed, available data indicate that those countries that import relatively more services also tend to export more of them.

Figures 3.2 and 3.3 show the results of an exercise correlating the exports and imports of services for a sample of 50 countries,

Table 3.6 Trade in services: the G-5 countries (million SDRs)

Country	Year	Shipment (+)	Shipment (−)	Passenger services (+)	Passenger services (−)	Other transport (+)	Other transport (−)	Travel (+)	Travel (−)	Labour income (+)	Labour income (−)	Property income (+)	Property income (−)	Other goods, services and income (+)	Other goods, services and income (−)
UK	1976	3271	1591	1172	584	2203	4028	2723	1653	—	—	603	462	5108	2400
	1986	2331	3189	2610	1905	2501	4073	6743	7410	—	—	1159	875	14044	4733
US	1976	2030	3800	1070	2220	3790	2140	4970	5950	170*	380*	3790	430	3100	1730
	1986	3670	9570	3030	5830	9280	5000	11010	14980	210	510	5830	910	7620	4220
Japan	1976	3450	2510	260	670	2520	5110	270	1440	80*	110*	150	690	2200	3910
	1986	5920	3740	570	1960	3170	6100	1240	6140	140	280	770	2750	6610	11850
Germany	1976	2530	2890	860	960	1010	1520	2860	7890	1230	1560	270	700	5210	6150
	1986	4600	3880	2010	2110	2540	2600	6710	17700	2440	3420	780	1640	13010	13940
France	1976	439	1029	—	—	4334	4063	3039	2963	714	793	175	508	8223	4267
	1986	5423	6576	—	—	5755	5045	8281	5552	1447	2490	586	1052	17227	9090

Source: IMF. Asterisks denote 1977 figures; plus signs, receipts; minus signs, payments.

Figure 3.2 Ratio of total services to GNP

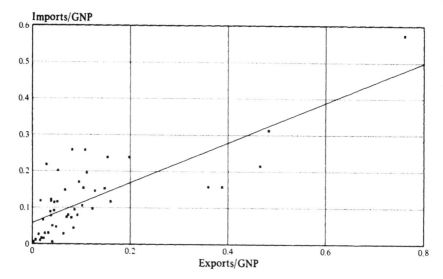

Figure 3.3 Ratio of selected services to GNP

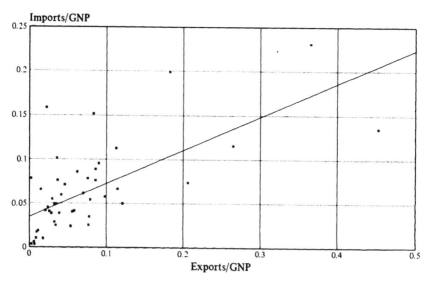

Selected services: Shipment; other transportation; travel; other goods, services, income.

36

including most industrial countries (1986 data). Because the volume of trade is affected by the size of the economy, in order to make the data comparable they have been normalized by GNP. Figure 3.2 relates imports to exports of services, both of which are expressed in proportion to GNP.[1] There can be seen a positive, although not very strong, relationship between the two ratios, which also include investment income. The statistics in Figure 3.3 exclude investment income. They are the aggregate of shipment, other transportation, travel and other goods, services and income. Again the relationship that emerges is positive. It is evident that some countries have a greater propensity to export services than others.

Of course, evidence supporting the view that those countries that import more services also tend to export more, and vice versa, does not mean that liberalization will necessarily improve export performance. Exporters, however, are likely to benefit from having access to cheaper and higher-quality services. An explanation of the positive relationship between imports and exports of services is that expansion of trade leads to 'intra-industry specialization'. Foreign competition need not displace domestic producers, but it may force them to specialize and differentiate their products. The flexibility of services must make them more receptive to 'product differentiation'.

Conclusion

Services are being used in increasingly more economic activities. They are probably used even more than available statistics indicate because it is difficult to obtain accurate measurement of service activities. Better telecommunication and transportation services have reduced transaction costs among countries, which in turn have facilitated the trade of more services. Whether a service can be traded without movement of the provider or client depends on available technology. There is nothing intrinsic or immutable that determines which services can be traded and which cannot.

Developing countries are apprehensive about opening up their economies because they fear that firms from a few industrial countries may dominate their national markets. Yet examination of the sectoral balances of the five major industrial countries reveals that there are more service industries in those countries which run deficits rather than surpluses. Data also show a positive relationship between exports and imports. Hence, not only could there be scope for developing countries to export to the markets of industrial countries, but their exports could also be made more competitive by trade liberalization, which improves access to cheaper and better services.

Note

1 The equations of the fitted lines in the two figures are as follows:

(a) $Y = 0.0579 + 0.5509X$
$R^2 = 0.6$

(b) $Y = 0.0375 + 0.3769X$
$R^2 = 0.45$

The estimated coefficients are significantly different from zero at the 99% level of confidence. The t-statistics are 8.44 and 6.25, respectively.

4

DISCRIMINATION VS REGULATION

The last two chapters have argued that because services are activities performed by persons, trade or transactions in services often require the movement of people. When movement is an integral part of trade, free trade can be achieved only when the movement of service-providers is unimpeded and their activities are unrestricted. These conditions, however, are hardly obtainable in practice. The first condition often comes into conflict with national interests and other non-economic objectives. The second condition may compromise the effectiveness of a government's regulatory system and competition policy.

The purpose of this chapter is to explore the meaning of 'free' trade in the presence of regulations designed to correct market failure or distortions. Governments regulate services for many reasons, some of which are blatantly protectionist. But, if some restrictions on the activities of service-providers do have an economic rationale, can there be a distinction between legitimate, or appropriate, and discriminatory regulatory measures? Moreover, is there a danger that liberalization among countries with distinct regulatory systems will give rise to unfair competition? What is the meaning of unfair competition in this instance? A government may be justified in intervening in service markets, but there are limits to intervention, since neither autarky nor laissez-faire is ever likely to be the correct policy.

The presence of legitimate regulatory controls, and the diversity of the various national systems, cast doubts on the appropriateness of attempts to liberalize services through the traditional approach of exchanging equivalent concessions. If national rules differ, there can be little of equivalence to be reduced or eliminated through reciprocal agreement. Moreover, the elimination of a few similar measures in industries, which are regulated by a plethora of other distinct rules and regulations, may have no equivalent effect in different national markets. More important, certain regulations may have a useful function in one country, yet be protectionist in another. As argued in this chapter, GATT will have to find an approach to liberalization which places more emphasis on the adoption of common rules. Such rules may range from detailed harmonization of regulatory systems to a more general undertaking to grant national treatment to foreign providers who can comply with national regulations. However, both harmonization and national treatment have their limitations, which are also identified in this chapter.

Why regulate?
In a world in which the only impediments to trade are border barriers (e.g. tariffs), reduction of such barriers improves the efficiency of resource allocation at both national and world levels. This means that every country becomes better off from liberalization. There are, however, three caveats to this proposition. First, liberalization must be non-preferential. Preferential tariff reduction, such as the formation of a customs union, may worsen national and/ or world welfare. Second, each of the liberalizing countries must be small and should not be able to influence world prices. Otherwise, the reduction of trade impediments by a large country may adversely affect its terms of trade (e.g., the ratio of export to import prices, or how much it pays in terms of exports for the goods it imports). Third, border barriers should be the only market distortions. If there are other distortions, trade liberalization need not improve economic efficiency.

Even if it is assumed that the first two conditions hold, the same assumption cannot be made for the third condition, since services may have to be regulated when markets do not function efficiently. While regulation may be justified by market failure, it is not always implemented for that purpose. Services, like other industries, are often regulated for political reasons, which may include protection of those industries that are perceived to be essential to a national economy. Governments have many motives when they intervene in the economy. This chapter examines those reasons that might necessitate government intervention to correct imperfect markets.

When markets do not function properly, improvement in allocative efficiency would require reduction in trade impediments *and* implementation of regulatory measures which impose no unnecessary costs (to be explained below) on service-providers. When tariffs are the only impediments to trade and given the caveats above, economic efficiency is maximized by reducing tariffs to zero. The zero-tariff equivalent for services is more complicated. From the perspective of a single country, the zero-tariff equivalent would comprise zero barriers and appropriate regulation, whose nature, however, also depends on policies in other countries. But two or more countries may be able to improve their economic efficiency further by adopting common regulations or by coordinating their policies in some other way. In contrast with the case for free trade in goods (provided that the caveats hold), the equivalent condition in services cannot be determined *a priori* because the efficiency or appropriateness of one country's regulatory policies depend on other countries' policies. This issue is examined more thoroughly in the following section. But first it is necessary to understand the nature of optimum or appropriate regulation.

The price of a good reflects the value attached to it by consumers only if consumers are well aware of its true qualities. When the information available to consumers is imperfect or incomplete, two problems arise. First, prices need not correspond to the assumed equivalent quality. Second, if consumers cannot distinguish among goods of varying quality, goods of higher quality will suffer as a result. This is the 'adverse selection' problem. The same thing may happen in a service market when consumers cannot distinguish among providers of different quality and competence. The providers know how good they are, but their clients may not. In all professional services there is an inherent asymmetry of information between consumers and providers. This is because in essence what consumers buy is professional knowledge and expertise. The aim of regulation in this instance is to improve the information available to consumers and minimize the extent of adverse selection.

Another related reason for regulation is the prevention of 'systemic failure'. This is a variation of the adverse selection problem whereby the failure of a service firm (e.g. a bank) may adversely affect the whole system or industry (see Kay, 1987 and 1988, and Goodhart, 1987, 1988a and 1988b). For example, when the public loses its confidence and there is a run on one or more banks, even sound, well-managed banks will be in difficulty because deposits are liquid while loans are illiquid. The prevention of systemic failure is the main reason why central banks act as lenders of last resort.

Regulation need not be exclusively imposed by the government. Markets themselves may develop self-regulatory measures. Producers of higher-quality products have an incentive to develop means by which to indicate their higher quality and differentiate them from inferior competitors. Strong market position often relies on establishing a reputation for quality. Self-regulation, for example, has been a major component of Britain's supervision of financial services. There are, however, several reasons why self-regulation is often supplemented by government supervision.

First, an increase in the amount of information available to consumers does not mean that they will necessarily be able to make better decisions, particularly if that information is very technical. Kay (1988) observes that information is voluntarily disclosed largely because it reveals little about the true quality of the service-providers. 'When there is actually something interesting to be disclosed, disclosure disappears very rapidly indeed' (p. 38). Moreover, markets would have a tendency to generate information whose objective may be to confuse and obfuscate rather than to enlighten.

Second, self-imposed rules and standards may not be legally enforceable. Professional and trade associations may have no legal right to prevent the operation of those who do not conform with the rules. It is even more difficult to enforce good behaviour in international markets that transcend national jurisdictions (e.g. Eurocurrency markets). The threat of tarnished reputation and consequent loss of business are the main disciplines in such markets. On the other hand, members of the same profession may be too lenient on their colleagues.

Third, private associations and professional clubs may develop such rules and standards that impede the entry of potential rivals into the regulated market. Privately generated rules may cartelize a market and reduce competition. Goodhart (1988a, p. 10) observes that 'some measure of oligopolistic practice provides often the cement that holds many of these clubs together'.

Cost of regulation

As already noted, there are several reasons which motivate government intervention. They do not justify it in every instance. As for any other economic decision, the benefits of intervention/regulation must be weighed against its costs. There are at least four kinds of costs. First, regulation may create a moral hazard. The regulations designed to protect consumers may actually reduce the quality of the regulated service. For example, if banks know that they will be bailed out by the central bank, they may attempt to undertake riskier investments. Public intervention may reduce the discipline imposed by the market. Slack management of quoted companies is punished by takeovers. But takeover of companies in regulated industries such as banking, broadcasting or communications often requires approval by the relevant government department or regulatory agency. Gaining approval can be a protracted affair, especially when the targeted company defends itself by claiming that the suitor has the unfair advantage of not having been subjected to the same restrictive performance requirements.

Another cost is that regulation limits what a firm can do, and it may therefore reduce competition within the market and by potential rivals wanting to enter that market. Theories of 'regulatory capture' also suggest that incumbent firms influence the nature of the rules in their favour (Stigler, 1971). Regulation may stipulate the state of affairs that should prevail in a market and the acceptable behaviour by firms within that market. Anything that disturbs the status quo may need prior approval or may instigate regulatory review. Continuous supervision is itself an impediment to change brought about by competition (see, for example, Veljanovski, 1987, on the regulation of broadcasting in the UK). Hence, regulation may inhibit competition and innovation of new services.

A third cost arises from the fact that consumers have different preferences. Regulation works by specifying required product features or the minimum acceptable level of quality. It reduces the variety available to consumers. Those who prefer a higher quality and are prepared to pay a higher price usually benefit as a result of regulation. Those, however, who are not willing to pay for the improved quality lose the option of buying a cheaper product at a lower quality. There can be no *a priori* presumption that the gains are always greater than the losses.

Finally, regulators need to compare the cost of compliance imposed on producers with the costs that are avoided by consumers. Compliance costs need to be lower than the cost savings made by consumers. Moreover, regulators ought to consider whether compliance costs will be permanent while the costs incurred by consumers are temporary and, thus, avoidable. Mistakes by consumers may be tolerable if consumers have the means of learning how to avoid repetition of the same mistakes. This requires that decisions are reversible (i.e., a consumer can opt for something different) and that the costs of mistakes are not prohibitively high (e.g., you do not want to have heart surgery performed by an unqualified person simply because he quotes the lowest price).

Efficient regulation
Ideally, efficient policies are directed at the source of market distortions. They seek to eliminate distortions at the least possible cost and without causing any unwanted side-effects. The fewer side-effects a policy instrument has, the more efficient it is. Similarly, appropriate regulation should be directed at the source of market distortion. There are several stages of government intervention. At the simplest stage the aim of regulation is to provide better-quality information to consumers so that they can choose the preferred mixture of quality and price. If additional information cannot help consumers, regulators may then specify the minimum acceptable level of quality or other required features and standards. Such product specifications must be kept to a minimum so that the range of available products is not unduly reduced. In addition to the provision of product information and the specification of product standards, regulators may stipulate how and by whom a good may be produced or a service provided. This happens when product characteristics cannot be easily defined.

The third type of regulation is especially prevalent in services. The first two types or stages of regulation apply to both services and goods. A service is a series of tasks. The end-result of a service cannot be inspected by the consumer before entering into a transaction. Often the only indication of the quality of the expected service is the credentials and reputation of the provider. Hence the qualifications of the service-provider are important when the transaction entails a long-term relationship and when the characteristics of the service output cannot be defined beforehand. Long-term relationships imply that decisions are likely to be irreversible. For example, whether a teacher has provided an adequate service is assessed after one leaves school and attempts to put into practice what one has learnt. Moreover, the nature of some services makes attempts to define their output particularly difficult. Some services are specifically intended to explore and provide previously unavailable information. They may be called 'exploratory' services and they exist because available information/knowledge is incomplete. They can be found, for example, in marketing, advertising, legal services and product design.

When regulation imposes restrictions on who enters a market or profession by requiring specific qualifications, the intention is to ensure the competence of the service-providers. Of course, satisfying entrance requirements is only an indication of capability to provide high-quality services; it does not guarantee that such services will actually be provided. If it is essential to test the competence of service-providers, then appropriate regulation should do just that. As argued later, regulations are discriminatory when they distinguish providers according to their origin or nationality rather than their competence.

In summary, regulation should ideally be designed to provide information, specify the minimum required product characteristics without limiting the range of available products, stipulate operating conditions which do not reduce competition and impose entrance qualifications that test competence rather than origin. Regulation is unnecessarily restrictive and blunt when it simply bans products, services and providers.

It should also be noted that the administration of regulation can itself be a source of inefficiency and market distortion. If the regulatory agency has too much discretion, there will be uncertainty as to what is acceptable in a particular market and the rules of engagement become ambiguous. For example, competition policy regarding mergers and acquisitions has been a particular issue of friction between supervisory agencies and the market. In Britain, the Secretary for Trade and Industry has the power to refer any takeover bid to the Monopolies and Mergers Commission. Precisely because his policy discretion is not bound by specific legal obligations, decisions concerning referrals are often seen as either unduly interventionist or improperly passive. A firm that attempts to acquire a rival cannot be certain of whether its bid will not be stopped.

But, although appropriate regulation would in theory require well-defined and transparent rules, in practice changing market conditions and the fact that rigid rules can be abused make it prudent for the regulators to retain some degree of discretion. The crux of any regulatory problem is the proper matching of incentives with information, so that the regulated firms are induced to act by disclosing appropriate information about themselves and by reacting to the relevant market signals. Because the matching of information and incentives cannot always be perfectly achieved, regulatory policies have in practice taken two basic forms, although there are many possible variations on those two themes.

At the one end of the regulatory spectrum there is the 'club' approach, whereby business regulates itself. Its main advantage is its flexibility in responding to changing market conditions and consumer needs. It can be supplemented by official supervision, whose object is to ensure the adoption of 'best practice' as this is developed by business. The regulation of financial services in Britain had – until the passing of the Financial Services Act 1986 – followed predominantly the club and the best-practice approach. The Act has much more formalized supervision, but considerable discretion and self-regulation continue to exist. For example, the Takeover and Mergers Panel is still a gentleman's club with no legal powers. It functions mostly by persuasion and peer pressure. As already discussed above, the major defect of the club approach is its tendency towards cartelization and the creation of entry barriers.

At the other end of the spectrum there is the statutory approach. Entry requirements and operating functions are formally codified. This approach may be fairer to potential competitors, but codification may reduce innovation because of its inherent inflexibility. Goodhart (1988a) argues that regulators have an incentive to overcodify so as to ensure that there is little likelihood of anything going wrong. An attempt to determine beforehand all the requirements and conditions that lead to acceptable firm behaviour inevitably results in overcodification.

Both the nature of the rules and the method by which they are implemented (e.g. regulatory discretion) may have a prohibitive effect on entry by new firms in a regulated market. This implies that even if all overt discriminatory measures against foreign firms are eliminated, entry into another country's market may still be difficult whenever regulatory requirements differ from those in the domestic market, or when firms are inexperienced in dealing with the administration of regulation in a foreign country.

Moreover, in the same way that those firms that survive market competition are those that are best adapted to market demands, the survival of the fittest in regulated markets also requires adaptability to the rules imposed by regulatory authorities. Different regulations breed different types of firms, and those firms that wanted to enter into another market might find that the structure they had developed was unsuitable for competing in that market. For example, if regulation is administered very informally, rather than on the basis of legally precise obligations, a foreign firm from a more legalistic system may realize that it could cope better with the new rules by hiring a person who came from the right school rather than by using its team of brilliant lawyers. Of course, inability to hire a suitable person and gain access to the informal network never fails to create the impression of unfair, if not discriminatory, treatment.

The discussion so far leads to several conclusions of relevance to unilateral or multilateral trade liberalization. First, when the purpose of regulation is to improve the functioning of markets, the criterion to use for authorizing service-providers is not their nationality but their professional competence. Second, regulatory authorities would inevitably maintain discretion over whom they authorize to operate in their national markets. Third, it follows that liberalization in a multilateral context would be an evolving process of negotiation, consultation, and rule modification. The idea that trade impediments could be eliminated by a one-off agreement belongs to the past. Services require continuous international review and consultation.

The following section considers how *bona fide* regulatory policies may be distinguished from discriminatory policies. To the extent that countries opt for discretionary regulation through the club approach, subtle discrimination may be difficult to detect and eliminate. It may also be difficult to define it objectively on the basis of quantifiable indicators. As argued in the following section, the fact that regulatory regimes differ across countries creates problems in assessing the competence of foreign providers.

Defining discriminatory policies

When trade occurs among countries whose markets are imperfect, it becomes even more difficult to define the nature of discriminatory measures because governments may justifiably attempt to prevent the spill-over of distortions from abroad. Trade may transmit distortions. From the point of view of a single country, such distorting spill-overs would be anything that would compromise the effectiveness of its own regulatory policies. Regulatory 'attenuation' occurs when foreign services are of lower quality or when foreign providers are not as competent as domestic providers. Attenuation is not necessarily 'bad' if the regulatory regime is over-restrictive. Hence, the term attenuation is merely descriptive and in this paper does not have the normative connotations which are often attached to it by those firms which are averse to foreign competition.

Trade among countries with different regulatory systems or regimes may also give rise to concerns about unfair competition, since different regimes are likely to have a different impact on competitive conditions in each country.

However, merely because some restrictions on trade may be justified, it does not follow that existing restrictions are justified. The purpose of this section is to examine whether there might be a case for trade measures; it does not seek to justify prevailing trade measures. Hence, it attempts to distinguish between discriminatory and legitimate/appropriate regulatory measures. This distinction ought to clarify what may be considered to be the objective of GATT negotiations. The EC has already submitted a paper suggesting the definition of guidelines on appropriate regulation, but it has not elaborated on what kind of policies it regards as appropriate.

One definition of discrimination is that equals, or those who provide equal goods and services, should be treated equally. A broader definition is that no policy should shift incentives in favour of a particular group. Discrimination is usually thought of in terms of different treatment of firms in the same industry. But any policy affects firms in all other industries to some degree. Implicit in interventionism, therefore, is a comparison between what protected firms deserve in relation to the unprotected ones. This indirect effect is not always appreciated by policy-makers. A complete definition of discrimination needs to take account of the effects of a policy on the whole of the economy. But this is probably an impossible task; instead of attempting to find the perfect definition, we might do better to try to find a workable definition.

There are several problems with those two broad definitions. First, any government policy, if it is to be effective, must affect incentives. Hence, any policy may favour/disadvantage some economic agents more than others, if only because some agents may be more capable of responding to that policy. Second, some form of induced change in incentives may raise social welfare or economic well-being. There immediately arises a conflict between the objective of improving welfare and that of extending equal treatment to all. Third, equal treatment may be unfair or inequitable if it ignores past treatment or current capability/handicaps. In order to account for the effects of past treatment, it is necessary to have a notion of what would have happened in the absence of government intervention. Thus, absence of intervention may also be discriminatory. In this sense, discrimination cannot be defined independently of the objective it wants to achieve. This requires a prior understanding of the ideal state of the world to be reached. In attempting to reach the ideal state, policies may have to redress the effects of past policies ad infinitum. A workable definition should avoid the problem of infinite regress and should not depend on concepts of an ideal state of affairs, which is itself very difficult to define.

A workable definition of discrimination is that a discriminatory policy distinguishes individuals and firms according to their national origin rather than other economic characteristics, such as their competence to provide services. The main reason why discrimination is bad is that if everybody does it nobody gains. If every country tries to promote the same industry, what will happen is that each country will cancel the effects of the policies of other countries. Some countries may gain in some industries, but it is unlikely that any single country could gain in all industries all the time. To retort that some country may, nevertheless, gain overall is to assume that that country will follow an optimal policy. But, first, it is difficult to determine optimal policies, since foreign policies change; second, predatory policies can easily escalate into trade wars beyond the control of the cool technocrat; and, third, constant interventionism imposes other costs on the domestic economy. A workable definition of discrimination should take account of the fact that there are many decision-making bodies (i.e. governments), whose policies may be incompatible. Hence, the purpose is to devise such rules that a trade system of many, independent, countries can function without friction. The objective is to make this system work, rather than to reshape the system to make it perfect. In addition, a workable definition should be capable of being implemented by all countries simultaneously. Promotion of origin or locality is self-defeating if all countries do the same. Avoidance of discrimination on the basis of origin is a workable rule but not ideal, since it does not account for past favouritism.

Non-discrimination on the basis of origin would still allow each country to have its own regulatory regime according to its preferences. There need not be any fear that regulatory regimes would be undermined so long as both foreign and domestic firms are subject to the same rules. This means that service-providers would have to move to the market they serve. In this case, non-discrimination would entail unrestricted entry and the granting of national treatment, assuming that providers are competent.

Moreover, no firm will be able to gain an unfair advantage if any one firm can enter any regime and enjoy the same privileges. And no government will be able to promote its own service industries at the expense of those of others if any other firm can enter the market and derive the same benefits. Therefore, when service firms can move across countries it is not necessary to harmonize regulations, since the existence of different regimes does not confer any exclusive advantages so long as foreign firms have the right to enter (i.e. the right of establishment) and operate (i.e. the right of national treatment) in any regime they wish. Nor are regulatory systems undermined so long as all firms are subject to uniform rules within each regime.

It would appear, therefore, that if the political will is there, it it easy to eliminate discrimination. There are, however, two types of problems. The first type includes all the obstacles relating to entry into new markets. The second type arises because trade may take place without the providers having to move from one market to another and also without them being under the same regulatory constraints.

Limited market access

Entry into a market may be impeded by several obstacles, which arise not because of any directly discriminatory measures but because of 'rule-incompatibility'. Different regimes may have different entry criteria and different regulatory methods, which may suit some firms better than others. For example, some national markets are legal monopolies. It is hard to argue that this is a case of trade discrimination when both foreign and domestic potential competitors are equally excluded. Entry requirements which presumably assess competence and ensure service quality may have a more restrictive effect on the providers from a particular location, even if these requirements are applied uniformly. For example, a country which requires its banks to maintain relatively large capital reserves would inadvertently hamper the authorization, and hence the entry, of banks from countries which require lower reserves. Such banks may have to establish subsidiaries with their own capital instead of simply opening branches. (See Feketekuty, 1988, for other examples of entry barriers.)

Even when entry requirements are uniformly applied, they may still be unnecessary for foreigners who may have already qualified in their own countries. It would be very cumbersome for a service-provider to pass the relevant national examination of every country in which it seeks to offer services. Not only is this kind of 'regulatory duplication' inefficient, but it is also an effective trade barrier because it imposes costs in terms of effort and time. For example, in 1988 the EC drafted a directive to liberalize the movement of professionals. The directive recognizes that professional training in different EC countries has many similarities, which can adequately be tested by any national authority. It permits additional testing and requirements for foreigners only on those aspects of professional training which are peculiar to a particular country (e.g. on the French personal tax allowances, but not on accounting principles).

The possibility of trade across frontiers without movement of providers also raises some difficulties. First, if providers operate under different rules, services may be of different quality. In this case, the appropriate regulatory response would be, at least in theory, to impose such measures as to make up the difference between the domestic, high-quality, services and those foreign services which are of lower quality. In practice, however, it would be difficult to impose 'differential' trade measures because this would first require the identification of the low-quality providers, estimation of the quality gap, and monitoring of a large system of differential measures of varying degree. It is also difficult to conceptualize such measures because services do not exist independently of their providers. If providers are based in a different regime, how can the quality of their services be improved by domestic rules? In banking, for example, there is either home-country or host-country control. There is no home-country-plus-the-difference control. For these reasons, differential measures are rather rare. Again, an exception is the recent EC directive on the liberalization of intra-EC movement of professionals. Each member country will recognize the others' diplomas, and it can require additional training only on matters relating directly to exclusively national rules in professions such as law and accounting.

Even if there are no regulatory differences across countries, it may still be necessary under certain conditions to restrict the cross-border trade of those services which may generate systemic risks. For example, in banking one of the methods of reducing the likelihood of systemic failure is the provision of deposit insurance, because it reduces the incentives for a run on a bank. Suppose two countries have exactly the same regulatory system and exactly the same deposit insurance scheme which, as is usually the case, covers only own nationals having domestic accounts. If one country allowed banks of the other country to provide services from across the border, its own nationals would not be covered by any one of the insurance schemes. The solution could not be a simple extension of the insurance scheme, because one country would provide insurance for banks over which it has no control and, more seriously, it would create a moral hazard for the other country's regulators. So what is a good policy for each country in isolation does not necessarily remain a good policy once trade commences. Hence, in services there are cases where unilateral liberalization is not beneficial. These instances do not hinge on 'optimum-tariff' considerations, whereby a large country may benefit from trade restrictions. Baltensperger and Dermine (1987, p. 93) argue that under these conditions there is a case for joint supervision and insurance. But if for some reason cooperation is not forthcoming, then each country may opt instead for a second-best policy requiring foreign banks to establish local subsidiaries before they can offer services to domestic consumers. For banks, this could increase their operating costs because it would be cheaper to operate from their home base or simply by establishing branches which do not require their own capital.

The banking example shows that even optimum regulations as seen from the perspective of a single country are not necessarily the most efficient trading arrangements. What is an efficient arrangement cannot be determined *a priori* for two reasons. First, the nature of an efficiency-increasing arrangement depends on the prevailing economic conditions and regulatory system of the potential partner. Second, there may be several possible arrangements. For example, two countries may agree to recognize each other's architectural qualifications even if training is different. Alternatively, they may decide to standardize training and testing procedures. There are costs and benefits in both options, so that it cannot be decided in advance which one is better.

It is worth noting that the EC has adopted the method of mutual recognition coupled with minimum harmonization as a means of liberalizing its internal market. Both mutual recognition and harmonization entail (gross) costs for the country that pursues optimum regulation. Harmonization changes its desired level/structure of regulatory supervision and, if the partner country has less strict rules, mutual recognition essentially reduces the effectiveness of its own system. Even such a country may be a net beneficiary if the gains from greater access into the partner's market outweigh the costs. Nevertheless, harmonization and mutual recognition are not unambiguously beneficial methods of liberalization in the same sense that tariff reductions are for a small country.

If optimum trading arrangements cannot be defined *a priori*, it follows that (a) any arrangement inevitably involves certain trade-offs and (b) whether an arrangement improves upon the status quo depends on the size of these trade-offs. Hence, there appears to be no simple principle for liberalization that would lead to globally free trade in services. Hindley (1988b) reaches a similar conclusion in a study examining the effect of national regulations on integrated world markets for services. But this does not mean that policy reform is impossible. The combination of free establishment of foreign providers, limiting entry requirements to tests of competence and granting national treatment to all foreign firms would much improve upon the present state of pervasive and opaque distortions. Trade officials should guard against concluding that there is no room for improvement simply because the global optimum escapes definition.

Appropriate regulation in GATT

Three conclusions arising from the preceding discussion are particularly pertinent to GATT. First, the complexity and diversity of regulations on the provision of services make it difficult to define equivalent concessions or concessions which have an equivalent effect. Moreover, regulations may have a legitimate economic role in preventing market failure.

GATT may more appropriately concentrate on eliminating policies which are incompatible with a system of trading nations. Such policies are those that seek to promote industry in one location at the expense of industries in other locations. Should all service-providers gain the right of establishment, these policies will be rendered ineffective. A typology of barriers to transactions in services is shown in Figure 4.1.

Therefore, in cases where proximity of providers and consumers is necessary, simple rules such as the granting of the right of establishment may be a more successful liberalizing strategy. Negotiating parties could, thus, focus on streamlining entry requirements.

Second, appropriate regulations may require that the regulatory agency retains some discretionary power and enforces what it perceives as best prevailing practice. Discretion, however, is diametrically opposite to transparency and would be suspected of covert discrimination, especially when best practice is developed by domestic firms. By contrast, extensive and transparent but rigid rules would defeat the purpose of maintaining supervision. They would also require detailed international agreements.

It is very unlikely that GATT signatory parties will agree to guidelines on appropriate regulation whose aim would be to improve the efficiency of government supervision. Sovereign governments would maintain that they have the prerogative to impose on their industry whatever costs they deem necessary. An agreement on appropriate regulation would require action similar to that of the EC Commission against Germany's beer-purity laws. Germany

Figure 4.1 A typology of barriers to transactions in services

I. **Non-traded services** (movement by providers necessary)

(a) *General and specific border restrictions:* These may cover the movement of goods, persons, capital or information. They may apply equally or differentially to foreigners and own nationals.

(b) *Restrictions/requirements regarding establishment:* A foreign firm could be forbidden from establishing commercial presence in its own right. It may be forced to establish a partnership. There may also be restrictions on the extent of ownership of or involvement in other domestic firms. Alternatively, it may be required to establish permanent presence even when it is not essential to the provision of a service. This category also includes the many and complex requirements concerning foreign direct investment.

(c) *Restrictions/requirements on business transactions:* Even when establishment is completely unregulated, a foreign firm may still be prohibited from transacting in some particular service or with a particular group of customers (e.g. restrictions on direct insurance).

(d) *Restrictions on inputs:* These involve local content and minimum value-added requirements and other rules on the employment of domestic personnel. There may also be restrictions on access to a market for an input or source of information. Alternatively, they may be required to rely on the services of local consultants, accountants and other experts.

(e) *Less favourable treatment:* Even when there are no outright restrictions, foreign firms may not be accorded full national treatment. Domestic firms, for example, may be subsidized or otherwise assisted (e.g. preferential procurement). It is quite common that foreign firms are subject to different fiscal and accounting requirements.

II. **Traded services** (movement by providers unnecessary)

(a) *Border restrictions:* Barriers to the trade of goods or information in which services may be embodied. Barriers to the cross-border sale of other services (e.g. insurance cover).

(b) *Use restrictions:* Consumers may not have the same legal protection or rights regarding the use of foreign services. For example, motor insurance purchased abroad may be inadmissible in a domestic court; architectural designs certified abroad may also be invalid under domestic rules.

(c) *Less favourable treatment:* Firms that purchase services from abroad or have their equipment serviced abroad may receive fewer tax allowances. They may also be treated unfavourably when bidding for public projects.

prohibited the import of beer with additives. German beer manufacturers were subject to the same rules as foreign manufacturers, so there was no direct discrimination. Yet the Commission argued that German restrictions were unnecessary, given that most countries allow additives without any apparent harmful effects. The essence of the Commission's argument was about the nature of proper regulation. The same position has recently been reiterated in a case regarding the purity of pasta imports into Italy.

It is worth noting that both Germany and Italy based their arguments on the supposedly proper way of defining those two products. For example, Italy argued that what is called pasta can be made only with hard durum wheat (which is grown mainly in Mediterranean regions). Given its poor record on dispute settlement, GATT is not the best forum in which to resolve disputes arising out of conflicting interpretations of proper regulation. One wonders what would happen if each GATT member attempted to define the characteristics of 'proper' services in terms of what they would allow to be provided by foreign firms.

Finally, it would be difficult to define the shape of permitted trading arrangements. For example, GATT Article XXIV specifies the conditions that free trade areas and customs unions should fulfil in order to be approved by GATT. The drafting of a similar article with respect to services would be a difficult task, since it would have to account for the numerous variations in the regulatory systems of potential partners. GATT may, nevertheless, attempt to reach a consensus on key common rules. An agreement on international standards in services may be feasible, given the precedents in telecommunications, air transportation and shipping. Such standards, however, generally define operating practices rather than rights of market access.

Conclusion

Regulations which restrict the activities of foreign service-providers are often imposed in the name of consumer protection. Often such measures have no other purpose than to protect domestic providers from international competition. However, to the extent that regulations have a legitimate economic function, certain restrictions on the entry of foreign providers into the domestic market may be permitted. In general, once foreign firms satisfy entry and competence requirements, regulatory objectives do not justify that they should be treated differently from domestic firms. However, because regulatory regimes vary, foreign firms may not be able to gain access and compete as effectively as other domestic firms in a market whose rules differ from those of their home market.

The liberalization of trade in services requires an ongoing commitment that can ensure that initial progress is not reversed. It is essential that such a commitment should involve a process of international consultation among trading countries because national authorities would maintain regulatory discretion. Unless countries harmonize all their rules in each service sector, there would always be the possibility of incipient trade friction because of 'rule-incompatibility'. There is no way that a trade negotiator could know in advance all of the aspects of another country's system that may become unfavourable to his own national firms after all the overt discriminatory measures have been negotiated away.

In order to ensure that the benefits of liberalization are not forfeited to covert discrimination, it is in the interests of those countries that join a multilateral agreement on services to establish an international surveillance and binding dispute settlement process for reviewing national regulations and resolving trade disputes. But such a process would succeed only if there were an agreement on binding trading principles and obligations.

Appendix to Chapter 4: Financial Deregulation in Britain

The British system of supervision of financial services has gradually evolved since the seventeenth century, when the Bank of England and the Stock Exchange were established. The objective of the Financial Services Act (FSA) 1986 has been to overhaul and consolidate the regulatory system so that Britain can retain its competitive position in world financial markets. Regulatory reform has been mainly a response to the challenges posed by the internationalization of finance.

The internationalization of finance has three major characteristics: (a) increasingly larger flows of funds across national frontiers; (b) greater presence of foreign financial institutions in the major financial centres;

and (c) increase in the size of assets owned by foreign residents and institutions.

Internationalization has been facilitated by: (a) trade liberalization and deregulation; (b) financial innovation, which has made available new and cheaper risk-spreading instruments; and (c) computerization, which has enabled electronic trading, reducing transaction costs and virtually eliminating response lag to changes in national markets.

The main features of deregulation as it has been implemented in various countries have been the following: (a) removal of interest-rate ceilings and of other credit restrictions; (b) reduction of constraints on the activities of financial institutions and of other legal boundaries that separate different types of institutions (e.g. retail and merchant banks); (c) abolition of exchange controls and other restrictions on capital movements; and (d) reduction of entry barriers into national financial markets (e.g. membership of stock exchange, market-making in government bonds).

In Britain deregulation commenced with the 'Big Bang' of 27 October 1986, which shifted trading of shares from the floor of the Stock Exchange to electronic trading. The main objectives of the regulatory reform have been (a) the breaking down of restrictive practices; (b) the consolidation and formalization of regulatory supervision; and (c) the strengthening of consumer protection.

There were several restrictive practices which impeded competition. Commissions on share transactions were fixed instead of being variable and freely negotiable. There was a separation between brokers and jobbers (market-makers). The Stock Exchange refused to allow corporate and foreign membership of the exchange. The FSA made all these restrictions illegal.

The financial industry used to be supervised by a system of separate self-regulating clubs, operating on the basis of informal and voluntary codes. Supervision was supplemented by occasional interventions from the Bank of England and the Department of Trade and Industry (DTI). The FSA established the Securities and Investment Board (SIB), which is responsible for the authorization and regulation of other Self-Regulatory Organizations (SROs), which in turn authorize individual financial institutions. Any institution which wants to provide services must first obtain authorization from the SRO responsible for its particular type of service. It may also be necessary to obtain multiple authorization. Even though the SIB is a private company, financed by the City, it can launch criminal prosecution. In addition to the SIB and SROs, the Bank of England continues its supervision of banks and the DTI has certain regulatory functions for life assurance and unit trusts and for investigating insider dealing. Lloyd's of London, which is in the wholesale (broking) insurance market, is outside the provisions of the FSA and has retained its own supervisory responsibility. The Takeover Panel is also separate from the FSA and is still operated as a gentlemen's arrangement without any legal powers.

Consumer protection has been strengthened by changes in the legal obligations of firms that offer services to private clients. These firms cannot promote their own products when they advise clients. There has also been established an insurance fund whose purpose is to provide compensation to the clients of firms that go bankrupt.

The regulatory system implemented by the FSA has been criticized for being too cumbersome and for resulting in overcodification of the permissible functions of service-providers. It has created several layers of supervision, each of which is costly to operate. It has also been argued that compliance with the new complex rules will impede the innovation of new financial instruments.

Sources
Clarke, M. (1986), *Regulating the City*, Open University Press, Milton Keynes.
Lomax, D. (1987), *London Markets after the Financial Services Act*, Butterworths, London.
Rybczynski, T. (1988), 'The Internationalisation of Finance and Business', *Business Economics*, vol. 23, no. 3, pp. 14–20.
Seldon, A. (ed.) (1988), *Financial Regulation or Over-Regulation?*, Institute of Economic Affairs, London.

5
LIBERALIZATION IN THE EUROPEAN COMMUNITY

The EC is engaged in a systematic effort to eliminate trade barriers among its member countries. This chapter examines how services are being liberalized and considers whether there are any lessons to be drawn that may be useful to other countries.

The EC approach to trade liberalization may not be perfect, but it is ambitious and comprehensive. It is also shaped by the special nature of the Community's institutions. As such, it does not provide a readily generalizable model for others to follow. The EC has overcome the obstacles arising from the existence of distinct regulatory systems by a combination of some regulatory harmonization and mutual recognition of national rules. Such policies are unlikely to be adopted by a wider, more diverse, group of countries.

However, there are elements in the EC's approach that can be adopted by other countries. For example, foreign service-providers could be granted the right of establishment under local rules. There could also be recognition of the regulatory competence of authorities in other countries.

The EC model is also interesting because of the way it has been adapted to deal with different problems in particular service sectors. The service sectors which have been selected for review in this chapter illustrate both the general principles of the EC model and its variations. These sectors are financial services, telecommunications, transportation and professional services. Financial services provide the basic theme of free cross-border trade, supplemented by the adoption of some common rules and mutual recognition. In professional services, member countries have been allowed to impose extra requirements on aspects of services that relate to peculiarities of national systems. The telecommunications industry is dominated by national monopolies and state-owned firms. With much difficulty the EC has been directing its efforts at increasing competition and opening up public procurement. Finally, in transportation the emphasis has been in the reduction of government control over entry into the industry. After summarizing and assessing developments in these sectors, the chapter concludes by examining the usefulness and applicability of the EC model to other countries.

Financial services
The Treaty of Rome, which established the EC, provides for the abolition of restrictions 'on freedom to provide services within the Community' (Art. 59) and of 'all restrictions on the movement of capital belonging to persons resident in Member States and any discrimination based on the nationality or on the place of residence of the parties or on the place where such capital is invested' (Art. 67). Despite the Treaty provisions, it has taken the Community almost thirty years to agree on some measures to open up trade of financial (and other) services across national frontiers.

Until the 1985 White Paper which elaborated the plan on the completion of the internal market, the Community had concentrated on enforcing the right of establishment for banks and insurance companies. Other financial services, such as securities and collective investments (unit trusts), were relatively neglected. The White Paper attempts to develop a comprehensive approach towards all financial services and also provides for the abolition of foreign-exchange controls that impede capital flows. At present, only Germany, the Netherlands and the UK have no exchange controls. Moreover, the White Paper aims at liberalizing the cross-border supply of services so that providers would not have to establish subsidiaries (which require authorization) in every member country.

The White Paper has adopted the following approach in bringing about free internal trade:
(a) harmonization of a number of essential prudential rules and standards of investor and consumer protection before all restrictions to the free supply of services are lifted;

(b) mutual recognition of national laws and regulations;
(c) home-country control of banks, insurers and other financial intermediaries; and
(d) elimination of measures that discriminate against non-national financial providers.

Within the general rubric of 'minimal harmonization' the Commission also includes differences in national systems that may 'distort competition'. The Commission has identified three areas for harmonization: (a) approximation of company taxation including tax base, allowances and rates; (b) prevention of tax evasion either by adopting a common withholding tax on interest and dividends or by information disclosure; (c) elimination of preferential tax provisions on investment in national securities and other financial instruments (Micossi, 1988, p. 220).

It is expected that by 1992 the Community will become better-off because financial services will be improved at least in two respects: 'greater operational efficiency, leading to the provision of financial services to the economy at lower costs; and greater allocative efficiency, assuring that savings flow to those uses with the highest expected real rates of return for any given risk level' (Monti, 1987, p. 498). Table 5.1 shows the credit and other regulatory controls that were in force at the time of publication of the White Paper. There is a north-south divide in terms of stringency of regulation, indicating that southern countries are likely to experience the most extensive changes in their financial markets. Not surprisingly, these countries have been allowed to phase out their restrictions during a longer transitional period. They have also succeeded in incorporating into the Community's proposals provisions for the reimposition of exchange controls in the event of a balance-of-payments crisis.

In January 1988 the Commission presented to the Council for approval the second coordinating banking directive. Its main provision is that banks would be allowed to operate anywhere in the Community under a single banking licence issued by the bank's home regulators and would be supervised by home regulators. The single licence would permit the establishment of branches (but not subsidiaries) without prior authorization by host countries. Subsidiaries, being separate legal entities, would still have to obtain authorization and would be subject to supervision by host-country regulators.

Table 5.1 Financial controls in the EC before project 1992

Country	A	B	C	D
West Germany	no	no	no	no
Britain	no	no	no	no
Benelux	no	no	no	no
Denmark	no	no	no	no
France	no	no	yes	yes
Italy	some	some	yes	yes
Ireland	yes	yes	yes	yes
Greece	yes	yes	yes	yes
Spain	yes	yes	yes	yes
Portugal	yes	yes	yes	yes

Source: Monti (1987).

A—Direct investments; property investments; capital transfers; short- and medium-term trade credits; transfers linked to insurance; transfers needed to perform services.

B—Buying shares in listed companies or units in unit trusts.

C—Issuing securities; buying unquoted securities; longer-term commercial credits.

D—Buying short-term securities; short-term financial credits; opening accounts with financial institutions.

The EC intends to harmonize prudential regulation with respect to minimum required capital, solvency ratios, large exposures, information on major shareholders, maximum investment in non-banking activities and deposit guarantees.

The single banking licence would be valid for a wide range of activities such as leasing, portfolio management and advice, and trading in securities both for the bank's own account and for clients. Any activity covered by the authorization granted in the home country is automatically valid in the host country, even if such an activity is not open to the domestic banks of that country. This will most likely have two important consequences. Initially, there could emerge a phenomenon of 'reverse discrimination' whereby banks in strict or restrictive regulatory regimes are disadvantaged in relation to banks from other countries. Subsequently, it is also very likely that the tradition of the 'universal bank' (prevalent in Britain, Germany and Holland) will spread to all of the Community by what may be termed as 'induced deregulation'. Either banks will lobby against national restrictions, or they will circumvent them by establishing subsidiaries in the least restrictive countries so as to operate through branches in their own domestic markets.

The proposed banking directive also makes an explicit reference to the treatment of non-EC companies. The approval of a licence for a non-EC bank would be conditional upon the granting of reciprocal rights by the bank's home country. Moreover, the Community expects that banks from all EC countries would receive the same treatment by third countries. In this way, the Community is using its size to force other countries to open up their markets to any EC bank. Chapter 8 examines more extensively the Community's request for reciprocity. Its objective is supposedly to induce the reduction of foreign trade barriers. But reciprocity is a dangerous weapon to use in trade diplomacy.

In insurance the problem is that countries allow the provision of services only by locally established firms. Trade across frontiers is, therefore, prohibited. For reinsurance (cover for insurance companies), however, establishment is not required, and in the EC reinsurance has been traded freely. The Treaty of Rome (Arts. 52–8) and two EC directives (1973, 1979) already provide for the freedom of establishment of insurance companies. As in banking, the Community has now directed its efforts at facilitating cross-border provision of services. Such cross-border provision of insurance is at present restricted to large risks (i.e. insurance for large companies). Again as in banking, no prior establishment effectively means no prior authorization by local regulators. Insurance companies will thus be subject to home-country regulation.

In June 1988, the EC Council approved new measures that would initiate home-country control for non-life, commercial risks by July 1990. The Community's current policy has been shaped by a landmark decision by the European Court of Justice (the Four Insurance case), which in 1984 ruled against Denmark, France, Germany and Ireland for prohibiting the sale of insurance cover by companies not authorized by them. The decision, however, was somewhat ambiguous because it stated that authorization could be unnecessary without specifying under what conditions it would be unnecessary. Hence, one interpretation of that ruling is that authorization would be required for reasons of consumer protection. Indeed, the new measures allow the sale of insurance only to large companies specified by size in terms of number of employees and turnover.

The rationale behind the new policy is that large companies are likely to have the required expertise in choosing the right cover from the right insurer. This means that consumers are assumed not to be able to appreciate the differences in contracts drawn by insurers from countries with different consumer protection legislation. The implication is that harmonization of provisions on consumer protection must precede liberalization of life and motor vehicle insurance. This conclusion raises two questions. Are differences in contracts and sale techniques so serious as to warrant blanket prohibition of all cross-border purchases of life insurance? And, why are countries with rudimentary consumer protection (e.g. Greece, Portugal) allowed to prevent trade on the grounds of consumer protection? These questions are considered again in the final section of this chapter.

Telecommunications
The Commission wants to open up the markets for broadcasting (TV and radio), satellite communications, value-added services on national telephone networks (transmission of data and other computer-based information), and telephone exchanges and other telecommunications equipment. Its approach consists of a combination of outright liberalization, mutual recognition of certification and other approval procedures for equipment and harmonization of technical standards. The EC's own estimates suggest that by the year 2000 the telecoms industry will account for up to 7% of the Community's GDP. It is currently 2% of the EC's GDP.[1]

Telecommunications provide a good example of how differences among national systems and their technical standards insulate national markets from international competition. Unilateral liberalization may not be very effective in the absence of bilateral or multilateral cooperation on standards, especially when standards change or new types of equipment become available. For example, the incompatibility of recently developed cellular technology prevents the use of mobile telephones in more than one EC country.

There are also cases where cooperation other than liberalization or standardization reduces operating costs. For example, the cost of leasing an international telephone line is reduced when there is single rather than multiple billing. Companies that lease international lines also claim that a major operating cost is the delay involved in detection of line faults and the requirement for multiple servicing.[2] Data networks (value-added services) are more useful the more

Figure 5.1 Regulatory barriers in broadcasting

Differences among national rules are often a source of restrictions to cross-border broadcasting. Rules on advertising differ substantially across Europe:

Austria:	Only 20 minutes advertising a day.
	No advertising on Sunday.
Belgium:	No medical advertising.
Denmark:	Only 5 minutes a day.
Finland:	No comparative advertising.
France:	No advertising for alcohol, the press, large retail stores.
West Germany:	No advertising concentrated in blocks.
	No advertising on Sunday.
Ireland:	No advertising for contraceptives.
Italy:	No comparative advertising.
	No employment-agency advertising.
Netherlands:	No advertising for mail-order or sweets before 8.00 p.m.
	No advertising on Sunday.
Norway:	No TV advertising.
Spain:	Low-alcohol advertising after 9.30 p.m.
Sweden:	No TV advertising.
Switzerland:	Only 20 minutes a day.
	No breaks within programmes.

Source: Annual Report and Accounts, 1987–8, Cable Authority, London.

extensive they are. But their expansion is inhibited by the fact that different national regulations raise administrative costs and might make impossible the establishment of integrated networks.

The Commission and the Council of Europe have drafted a directive and a convention, respectively, to regulate the international transmission of television programmes. A major objective of these draft regulations is to implement common practices on the acceptable time-length and type of advertising and on programme content so that more air-time is given to programmes made in Europe and to prevent the transmission of pornography. Those European countries that restrict advertising are afraid that the advent of satellite television will undermine their domestic status quo. These countries are Germany, Holland, Belgium and the Nordic countries. Figure 5.1 shows the broadcasting rules that prevail in Europe.

Cross-border broadcasting has been made possible by satellite technology and the laying of cable networks. Governments so far have been able to enforce their regulations by restricting the operations of the companies that maintain the local cable networks. However, technology miniaturization of dish antennae is increasingly enabling more private individuals to receive signals directly from satellites. Governments are thus losing their control. The purpose of the EC directive and the Council of Europe convention is to shift regulatory responsibility from the country where broadcasts are received to the country where they originate.

The opponents to these plans have been those countries in which advertising has been relatively free (e.g. Britain, Ireland, Luxembourg and Spain). The Independent Television Association in the UK has estimated that if the proposed restrictions on advertising came into effect, they would increase the cost of UK television airtime by 5–10%. Harmonization which seeks to protect the broadcasting traditions of particular countries is likely to impose costs on third countries.

Britain, which has most of the satellite broadcasting companies, also opposes plans by the EC to specify a quota for non-EC feature programmes. The Commission has proposed that 'at least 60%' of all programmes should be from EC countries. Such restrictions would have a detrimental effect on cable channels that specialize in screening films, the majority of which are American.

There could be at least two reasons why the EC is attempting to harmonize national practices. The first is that unregulated satellite TV will be motivated by commercial profit without having any regard for local culture. This is the perennial issue of the corruptive power of television. Hindley (1987) argues, however, that the preservation of cultural integrity does not necessarily justify an outright ban on what viewers can watch in private; it merely justifies public assistance being given to cultural channels.

The second reason may be the protection of the advertising revenues of state-controlled stations. In April 1988 the EC Court of Justice ordered the Netherlands to lift its restrictions on Dutch-language advertising carried by foreign cable channels. It also ordered the removal of the ban on direct targeting of Dutch audiences by advertisers. Since advertising was already allowed on Dutch television, restrictions on advertisements carried by foreign cable operators were evidently discriminatory. However, discrimination is harder to detect when domestic channels are subject to the same restrictions.

Figure 5.2 Fragmented telecommunications

EC estimates suggest that by the year 2000, the telecom industry will account for up to 7% of the Community's GDP against 2% today. But preferential public procurement, diversity of technical standards and other restrictive measures have distorted trade so that intra-EC exports in 1986 were ECU 803 million while extra-EC exports were ECU 1,545 million. By contrast, more than 60% of EC merchandise trade takes place among member countries.

Restricted trade gives rise to price differentials. It is estimated that in 1987 telecom users in Britain and France paid $225–250 per line for digital equipment, while in Germany the price was $500 per line.

The fragmentation of the telecom industry in Europe and the existence of multiple, officially sponsored R&D activities also contribute to higher costs because they prevent manufacturers from reaping economies of scale. In the US the price per line of digital equipment is estimated at $100–150. The lower price reflects both the effects of more competition and lower production and maintenance costs resulting from economies of scale.

Source: Pelkmans and Winters (1988), pp. 51–3.

In November 1988 member countries of the Council of Europe decided to adopt its draft convention. That decision was somewhat surprising because in fact members of the EC implicitly forced the Commission to modify its own directive so that it becomes compatible with the convention. This development must be welcome because the convention merely asks its signatories to increase the European content of their television programmes without specifying a minimum limit.

In telephone and satellite communications the Commission has proposed extensive liberalizing measures. The proposals include the opening of national markets for telecommunication services so that value-added services on existing networks would be open to EC-wide competition. The opening up of national markets involves the elimination of discriminatory measures and the harmonization of the different administrative practices that prevent the establishment of integrated data networks and the leasing of international telephone lines. National telecommunication authorities would be allowed to maintain their exclusive rights only in the transmission of voice messages (telephone calls). Figure 5.2 presents some estimates of the effects of segmentation of telecom markets.

The Commission also intends to draw up guidelines for the application of EC competition rules. One of the problems in achieving greater competition is that in most EC members the market is a legal monopoly and/or the main operator is a state-owned company. Therefore the Commission wants tariff structures to be cost-related in order to curb discriminatory pricing. It also wants greater transparency in the financial relations between governments and state-owned telecom authorities so as to prevent illegal subventions. Differences among national VAT systems are also perceived to be giving rise to uncompetitive price differentials. In some countries telecommunications are VAT-exempt. Hence, the Commission favours the application of harmonized VAT rates by all countries.

An important aspect of the Commission's proposals concerns the liberalization of sales of telecom equipment. Trade in such equipment is restricted by national monopolies, preferential procurement and incompatible technical standards. Relying on Art. 90 referring to monopolies, the Commission wants to abolish monopoly rights, ensure that procurement is non-discriminatory, harmonize technical standards where necessary and eliminate regulatory duplication by mutual recognition of equipment approved by other member states.

There is consensus among member countries that the markets for terminal equipment and value-added services should be opened up. There remain, however, differences on the appropriate policy towards third countries and whether the EC should be responsible in forming a common external policy. Commission officials have stated that the EC intends to make access by foreign companies conditional upon reciprocal concessions by the governments of their countries. Japan is especially targeted for bilateral pressure. The Commission regards the EC's bilateral deficit with Japan in telecommunication equipment as evidence of Japanese restrictive practices.[3]

Another area of contention is the development of satellite communications. Until recently some international satellite services have been exclusively provided by national authorities and other legal monopolies (e.g. voice communication). This situation, however, is now changing. In April 1988, the Department of Trade and Industry announced its intention to license up to six additional operators to compete with the duopoly of British Telecom and Mercury. It also approved a joint venture between BT and Kokusai Denshin Denwa (KDD), Japan's largest provider of value-added services. The objective of the venture is to promote the transmission of business services between Japan and Britain. It is worth noting that KDD already faces competition in its domestic market by International Digital Communications, which is partly owned by Cable and Wireless.

The significance of these developments is that if the EC attempts to implement a restrictive common external policy, as in banking, it will have an immediate negative impact on the more advanced countries. Not only do these countries have a lot more to lose in their domestic markets, but they are also the likely target of foreign retaliation, which would be directed against their companies operating in the foreign markets.

Transportation
More than 80% of intra-EC trade is transported by road (Pelkmans and Winters, 1988, p. 51). The value of total EC road haulage is estimated at approximately ECU 470 billion (£325 billion). About three-quarters of intra-EC haulage is controlled by bilateral quotas, which specify the number and type of permitted lorry journeys. Not only do these quotas stifle competition from other member countries but they also cause much additional waste. The EC has estimated that such restrictions force one in three lorries travelling between member states to go empty. According to Dow Chemical, up to a quarter of the 200 lorries that daily leave its factories in Benelux are forced to return empty from their EC delivery points.[4]

After protracted deliberations, the EC Council agreed in May 1988 gradually to abolish bilateral quotas and other licences by 1990. Member countries have not yet agreed on a firm plan to allow cabotage-transportation by non-national carriers within the territory of a third country. The major stumbling-block to the May agreement was Germany, which had been insisting that liberalization had to be preceded by fiscal and other regulatory harmonization. German hauliers, which are highly taxed and tightly regulated, would be vulnerable to competition from less controlled operators. Holland and Germany have more than a third of the total EC market, perhaps reflecting the importance of Rotterdam as the biggest port in the world and of Germany as the biggest exporter in Europe.

The Commission's proposals, some of which have not yet been approved, go beyond mere elimination of quantitative restrictions. The other two major aspects are technical standardization and fiscal harmonization. Both are intended as a means of preventing 'competitive distortions'. Technical standardization concerns (a) the type of lorries (dimensions, etc.), (b) driver qualifications and working conditions (e.g. how often and how long drivers have to take a rest-stop), and (c) the criteria for levying vehicle taxes (e.g. unladen weight, number of axles, engine capacity). Fiscal harmonization refers to vehicle tax, road usage tax, VAT and fuel excise tax. The proposed plans also include a fiscal innovation which provides for the collection of road tax by the country whose roads are being used (i.e. in EC parlance, the 'territoriality' principle) instead of the country of registration of the vehicle (i.e. the 'nationality' principle). This is in principle correct but raises the problem of how to determine road usage in a market without frontiers.

It is also worth noting that the Commission's package, on Germany's insistence, mentions a series of social and infrastructural measures to alleviate the costs borne by those regions that would experience increased traffic. These measures may be designed to compensate for negative externalities, or they may be side-payments for extracting Germany's consent.

Once again the approach to integrating the internal market involves a mixture of abolition of discriminatory measures, harmonization and standardization. Unlike air transportation, the fairly competitive conditions in road haulage did not prompt the Commission to propose additional measures designed to inject competition into the industry.

In December 1987 the Council reached an agreement on new policies regarding air transportation. The agreement was delayed by a dispute between the UK and Spain over the status of Gibraltar's airport. The agreement was not path-breaking. It is aimed at containing anti-competitive and collusive behaviour rather than at deregulating the market.

The December accord does not directly abolish bilateral agreements, such as capacity and revenue-sharing, fare agreements on permissible discounts, joint ventures in computer reservation systems and arrangements on landing slots and baggage-handling facilities. The Commission has instead chosen to impose stricter competition rules so that even if such agreements are permitted, they do not discriminate against third-country airlines. The Commission has also given itself the right to investigate and penalize anti-competitive behaviour.

The new air transportation regime is likely to reduce discrimination of carriers that are already in the market, but it does not have sufficient power in opening up markets, especially for third-country airlines. For example, in August 1988 the Commission fined Sabena for abusing its dominant position in Belgium by restricting access to its Saphir computer reservation system by Ryanair Europe.[5] But it did not react to complaints by Aer Lingus that Italy refused to allow it to fly to Milan via Manchester.[6]

Stricter application of competition rules would contain excessive and discriminatory pricing. Recent evidence suggests that the industry is inefficient, with high operating costs. It could be argued, therefore, that one way to reduce high costs would be the deregulation and opening up of the industry to competition from new, more efficient and, perhaps, bigger airlines. Pryke (1987) found that, for comparable flights, European airlines spend 50% more than American airlines. In particular, administrative overheads and ground costs are 365% and 315% more than those incurred by American airlines. In 1982, before deregulation was fully implemented in the US, American pilots earned 37% more than the average manual wage, while in France (Air France) it was 670% and in Holland (KLM) and Italy (Alitalia) 590% more than the average manual wage. Part of the inefficiency can be attributed to the unnecessary duplication and diseconomies of small scale arising from the insistence of governments to maintain national carriers (Pelkmans and Winters, 1988, p. 50). Witness the furore over the bid by SAS for British Caledonian in 1987–8. It remains to be seen whether in a unified Europe governments will tolerate rationalization of the industry and, perhaps, a takeover of their national airline.

Professional services

The freedom of movement of labour and the right of establishment are guaranteed by the Treaty of Rome in Articles 48–51 and Articles 52–8, respectively. It would appear, therefore, that there is no need for additional directives to facilitate the trade of professional services such as accountancy, surveyance, etc. In reality, cross-border movement is not free because there are entry requirements for those who want to practise in different national markets. As noted in the preceding chapter, even when there are no overt or intentional/deliberate discriminatory measures against foreign service-providers, the cross-border flow of providers may be impeded because different regulatory systems have disparate qualifying requirements for assessing competence to offer services. Services such as medicine, law or accountancy are heavily regulated in all EC countries.

Before the publication of the White Paper, the Commission sought to facilitate the movement of professionals by harmonization of the different national entry requirements and qualifications. Even though agreements were reached on doctors, nurses, dentists, midwives, pharmacists, veterinarians and architects, the process proved to be too slow and cumbersome. The White Paper marks a shift in the Commission's approach, emphasizing mutual recognition of diplomas rather than harmonization. In June 1988, the EC Council agreed on new measures that would facilitate the movement of lawyers, accountants, patent agents, surveyors, engineers and teachers. The new arrangements provide for mutual recognition of diplomas so that these professionals do not have to requalify in every EC country in which they wish to practise.

Recognition, however, may not be immediate. Members of the legal and the legally related professions (lawyers, accountants, patent agents) may be required to take aptitude tests and practise for up to three years before they can qualify. The reason is that legal and accounting conventions differ across the EC, so that qualification under one system need not guarantee ability to practise under another. Within the logic of regulation this provision is in principle correct, because it presumably seeks to determine competence only for those aspects of a profession which are peculiar to a country's system. It thus avoids regulatory duplication. However, it is still an open question whether aptitude tests are necessary and whether they will not be biased against foreigners.

As expected, mutual recognition has already injected more competition into the most heavily regulated professions and countries, producing some interesting results. For example, German rules stipulate that a lawyer must be a member of the bar of the town where a case is heard. This 'territorial exclusivity' rule prevents German lawyers from addressing courts other than those of their town or those of which they are members. In February 1988, the Court of Justice declared that a lawyer from another member state cannot be subject to these rules because this would restrict trade in services. German rules effectively discriminate against their own nationals. One wonders how long German lawyers will tolerate this unfavourable treatment in their own country. Mutual recognition opens up regulatory competition and puts pressure on the regimes with the stricter rules.

Lessons from the EC approach to liberalization

The EC is trying to unify its internal market through a mixture of outright elimination of discriminatory measures and minimum harmonization of national regulations. It has allowed member countries to retain some policy discretion in determining the structure of their individual regulatory systems. The abolition of border and other entry restrictions, coupled with home-country control and mutual recognition of that control, will most likely instigate regulatory competition resulting in regulatory uniformity at the level of the least restrictive system. Is this the right approach to liberalizing trade in services and one worthy of imitation by other countries?

In theory, had the EC countries been maintaining optimum regulation according to their needs and preferences, mutual recognition would result in 'induced deregulation', which would disturb the optimum balance of their economic management. So why have they accepted to be bound by the constraints of mutual recognition? There are several possible answers to this question.

First, none of them has really efficient regulation. National regulatory systems are still over-restrictive and discriminatory. Second, the EC structure in general, and the internal market initiative in particular, are a huge system of trade-offs. A country may lose out in one sector but gain in another, or be compensated by side-payments in terms of regional or structural aid. Since the internal market initiative comes as a package, it needs to be evaluated as a package. It is doubtful, however, whether any member country has attempted a comprehensive cost-benefit analysis of all possible effects on its national markets. Third, member countries may have been induced to consent to the provisions of the various directives as a result of the Single European Act, which has made majority voting possible on internal market issues. Fourth and most likely, the task of harmonization of all national regulations would have been herculean if not impossible. Finally, the Community would not have been able to wrest all policy discretion from national governments. The transfer of substantial economic decision-making to Brussels would hardly have been welcomed politically.

Political pragmatism may explain the approach adopted by the EC. But its economic rationale is still open to question. There is much evidence indicating that economic efficiency within the Community will be substantially improved after 1992 (Padoa-Schioppa, 1987; Pelkmans and Winters, 1988). Yet doubts have been expressed as to whether the current approach is the best method of integrating the internal market. Hindley (1987) has criticized the view that harmonization of prudential regulations must precede trade liberalization. There is a danger of limiting consumer choice and of creeping re-regulation as the rules determined by the Council are given an increasingly wider interpretation by Brussels technocrats. He suggests that the market itself will show whether regulation is valued by consumers. As long as existing national regulations provide at least a minimum level of consumer protection, there may not be a need for further harmonization and implementation of Community-wide rules. Nor does it necessarily follow that because protection provisions differ, consumers will be unable to understand the significance of such differences.

There is also a disturbing duality in the Commission's thinking. On the one hand, it accepts and encourages competition among regulatory regimes; on the other, it seeks to impose a 'level playing-field' by harmonizing tax systems and approximating tax rates (e.g. VAT, excise taxes, company taxation, other fiscal charges). The competitive impact of home-country control is blunted by this levelling of taxes. The Commission has not explained why it regards tax differences as 'distortions of competition' while regulatory differences are considered acceptable. Moreover, if countries are forced to adopt the same tax systems, they will forgo the use of an important policy instrument. Other things being equal, fiscal instruments will be much less effective in a unified market. But other things are never equal and tax measures may be a useful policy instrument in correcting market imperfections or in influencing consumer behaviour. The Commission has not made any distinction between the possible use of taxes as discriminatory measures and as market-correcting measures. Corrective measures may indirectly affect trade but need not discriminate on the basis of nationality.

The Commission's concern about a level playing-field raises the issue of whether there are any valid economic reasons for implementing harmonization before trade liberalization. In a freely trading world with many countries, regulatory competition may lead to systemic failure. But in how many services is the spectre of systemic failure a reality, and how likely is it that the emergence of European 'Bahamas and Cayman Islands' will remain undetected and unchecked? In other cases where technical standards are essential (e.g. telecommunications), harmonization is an integral part of liberalization. Entry into markets with different standards can be achieved only by adopting the same standards. Hence, harmonization is necessary when there are standard incompatibilities, entry requirements and the danger of systemic failure. Otherwise, provided that there is a minimum level of consumer protection, competition among regimes may actually be welcome.

If the Community managed to harmonize all regulations, would it be able to amend them in response to changing market conditions? An important consequence of home-country control/mutual recognition is that it is easier for one country to update and overhaul its regulations than it is for the Community, which has to go through a process of consultation, bargaining and approval involving twelve countries. Therefore, harmonization at the Community level may facilitate trade initially, but it is likely to result in some degree of institutional and regulatory rigidity afterwards. The static cost of possible competitive distortions from non-harmonization must be weighed against the dynamic cost of regulatory rigidity from harmonization. At best, the degree of necessary harmonization must still be regarded as an unsettled issue.

Can the EC model be replicated?
Given the reservations about harmonization, can the EC model be adopted by other countries and systems, especially by GATT? This question is more thoroughly explored in the following chapter, which examines the GATT system and the difficulties of adopting the EC approach. Even if the EC model is good, it must still be asked whether it is a model other countries can imitate. In understanding the difficulties that other countries may have in following the EC's approach, consider again the three basic elements in the Community's policy: (a) abolition of discriminatory measures concerning trade and establishment; (b) mutual recognition and home-country control; and (c) minimum harmonization of prudential rules.

Home-country control and mutual recognition are 'open-ended' principles. The general rule embodied in them is that each member country will respect the legitimacy of the regulations and laws of other member countries, provided that state security, public morals and national culture are not compromised. The problem with open-ended principles is that they may be subject to conflicting interpretations. For example, suppose that the UK suddenly decides to abolish all restrictions to practising law. Prospective solicitors and barristers are allowed to practise without having to join their professional organizations. Could Germany argue in this instance that its obligation under the Treaty is to recognize British regulations but that it has no obligation to accept a British lawyer who is not a member of the British Bar and thus not subject to any regulations? Does mutual recognition extend only to persons who are subject to a national system of rules, or does it also cover persons who are not subject to any particular system of rules? This example shows that because open-ended principles may be given different interpretations, they usually need an arbiter, a court, to resolve conflicting interpretations.

The European Court of Justice has often been described as the staunchest defender of free trade within the Community. The reason is that the EC constitution is one of only two constitutions in the world which guarantee the freedom of trade across national borders for individuals. The other is the Swiss constitution (Petersmann, 1988). It is worth noting that whereas the Swiss constitution guarantees the freedom to trade with any country, a Community national can trade freely only with other member countries. It is unlikely that the EC would have progressed to its present stage without the Court's rulings on cases brought by individuals, which have often forced unwilling governments to open up their markets. It is also unlikely that the principle of mutual recognition will succeed in facilitating trade unless there is a court to give it substance. Yet even the Court has occasionally ignored economic arguments in reaching its decisions, even when it was within its remit to consider such arguments (e.g. the Four Insurance case).

The EC experience shows, above all, the difficulty of liberalizing cross-border trade in services. It also shows that there is no single, correct and simple solution to the problem of determining the proper combination of harmonization and home-country control. The nature of the proper combination is likely to depend on who the trading partners are. Both harmonization and home-country control limit the range of potential partners because they are more likely to be implemented and sustained by partners with similar economies and strong political ties. Moreover, given that these two principles would require frequent regulatory review and amendment, they would be more appropriate for a small group of countries with willingness to cooperate closely.

The EC model also indicates the usefulness and, perhaps, necessity of supranational institutions, such as a review body or committee and an arbitration body to ensure that, where countries retain policy discretion, they do not abuse it. For example, EC countries have retained the power to impose differential measures in professional services (e.g. further training and aptitude tests). Given that the ability to provide services depends on gaining access to a market, the objective of the other supranational body would be to prevent abuse of monopoly power and safeguard competition (e.g. the EC's policy in telecommunications and air transportation).

All of these difficulties associated with the opening of trade indicate that a relatively easier step is probably the granting of the right of establishment and national treatment, provided entry requirements are satisfied. Each country could maintain its own regulatory system. Cross-border trade of services might be restrained, but the movement and establishment of foreign providers should not cause any regulatory problems. If all firms in each country are subject to the same rules, there would be no need to worry about the effects of the supply of services by providers of different national origin. It would, however, be necessary to ensure that entry requirements and subsequent treatment are non-discriminatory, based on competence rather than origin.

Conclusion

The EC's internal market initiative is primarily an attempt to integrate the economies of its member countries. As such, it has no formal external objectives. Of all the directives that have already been approved or are currently under consideration, only the banking and financial services directives make a specific mention of the treatment to be accorded to foreign service firms operating in the EC. These directives define reciprocity as a prerequisite for the authorization of foreign banks and the granting of permission to do business across the EC.

The concept of reciprocity and its implications for the Community's external relations are more extensively considered in Chapter 8. One aspect of the reciprocity clause is that third-country banks would be prevented from engaging in cross-border trade. This raises the issue of the legal standing and rights of third-country firms. Article 58 of the Treaty of Rome provides for non-discriminatory treatment of foreign firms which are established in a member country. Whether reciprocity requirements contravene Article 58 cannot be resolved within the context of this paper. But the fact that reciprocity has become a major issue in the Community's external commercial relations proves that unless there is an undertaking to extend national treatment to locally established foreign service-providers, governments would always devise schemes that favour their own firms.

The problem of how to treat third-country firms is indicative of the difficulties that GATT members are likely to face in their attempts to reach an agreement on liberalization of service trade. As the next chapter shows, this issue has not even been considered in the GATT negotiations.

Notes

1 *The Sunday Times*, 24 April 1988, p. D9.
2 Statement by the Director of Volvo Product Developments at a *Financial Times* conference on telecommunications, London, 28 June 1988.
3 Statement by Michael Carpentier, Head of the EC's Telecoms Director-ate, at a *Financial Times* conference on telecommunications, London, 28 June 1988.
4 *The Financial Times*, 14 March 1988, p. 2.
5 Ibid., 27 July 1988, p. 3.
6 Ibid., 7 June 1988, p. 4.

6
SERVICES IN GATT

The question of inclusion of services in GATT has resulted in a North-South division. Developed countries want the reduction of restrictions on both cross-border trade and movement of service-providers. Developing countries are apprehensive of what they perceive as a potential loss of policy autonomy over their economies. This chapter first reviews the state of the debate and then, using concepts developed in previous chapters, examines the various proposals on liberalization of services. It concludes that, in view of the complexity of services, liberalization would be an ongoing process requiring binding commitments by participating countries. The following chapter, which examines the concerns of developing countries, suggests that it is in their interests to participate actively in an international agreement on services.

Bringing services to GATT
The current 'Uruguay' round of GATT trade talks was launched at Punta del Este, Uruguay, in September 1986. The Punta del Este Declaration revealed the extent to which delegates disagreed on whether GATT was the proper forum and whether it had any competence in considering services.

On one side, the US, supported by Canada, Japan and the EC, insisted on extending GATT's mandate to services. On the opposite side, India and Brazil, supported by other less developed countries, objected to any intrusion by GATT into services. In their view, services were already considered by other international organizations, national policy prerogatives could not be subject to negotiation and GATT had first to complete the liberalization of trade in goods before getting side-tracked into other 'less important' issues. Opposition to services by developing countries was expressed as early as the 1982 GATT Ministerial meeting. Throughout the meeting the US exerted strong pressure on other delegates to instruct the GATT Secretariat to undertake formal studies on barriers to trade in services. The Ministers were only able to agree that interested contracting parties could, if they wished, undertake national studies on services, which they could circulate to other members. Only seventeen countries submitted such papers, which showed, more than anything else, the complexity, diversity and incomplete understanding of services. Most papers proposed some form of multilateral agreement. The US submission was the most extensive and ambitious. It advocated a framework of principles which could safeguard non-discrimination, national treatment and the right of establishment. The subsequent discussions on those papers, during 1984–5, were informal and did not lead to any agreement. At a meeting of the GATT Council in November 1985 it was decided to formalize the group which was discussing the papers. The group was chaired by Ambassador Felippe Jaramillo of Colombia, and its mandate was to prepare the basis for negotiations during the new GATT round.

The decision to formalize the Jaramillo Group did not lessen opposition by the developing countries. The tone of the American side became more confrontational. Clayton Yeutter, the US Trade Representative, was quoted as saying, 'We simply cannot afford to have a handful of countries, responsible for 5 percent of world trade, dictate the destiny of a large number of countries who deal with 95 percent of that trade.'[1] The US also threatened to withdraw its tariff preferences for developing countries if they continued to block the inclusion of services in the new round.[2]

At the Punta del Este Ministerial meeting the Jaramillo Group was unable to make any recommendations. There was an unbridgeable divergence of opinion between the US, Canada, Japan and the EC on one side, and most prominently Brazil, India, Egypt and Argentina on the other. Brazil and India could not even accept the need for multilateral negotiations on services, let alone recognize

GATT's competence. There was, however, a considerable number of developed and developing countries which favoured a compromise. They were willing to discuss services as long as they did not distract from other issues. They were also willing to accept that there was a case for subjecting trade in services to GATT scrutiny; they did not, however, expressly advocate a framework of principles. Part of the problem of including services in GATT was that there was no clear understanding whether existing GATT rules could accommodate services or whether it would be necessary to amend the treaty. The question whether GATT would need to be augmented was left unanswered by the Punta del Este Declaration.

The Punta del Este meeting established a Group for Negotiations on Services (GNS), which was different from the Group for Negotiations on Goods (GNG). The expressed intention was to enable the negotiations on services to proceed on a separate track – the 'twin-track' approach. This approach was a compromise that removed the obstacle to the launch of a new GATT round. However, as became evident later on, no substantive issues had been resolved by following the twin-track approach. If anything, it became a source of further friction and contention because the legality of the GNS was still ambiguous.

Each side has interpreted the Declaration as supporting its own point of view. The Declaration states that the negotiations 'shall aim to establish a multilateral framework of principles and rules' in order to achieve expansion of trade and progressive liberalization. It also states that trade expansion and liberalization are viewed as 'means of promoting economic growth and development'. Moreover, a framework of principles is expected to 'take into account the work of other relevant organizations' and to 'respect the policy objectives of national laws and regulations'.

The part of the Declaration on services was made by the Ministers not on behalf of the contracting parties but in their capacity as representatives of sovereign states. As a result, Brazil and India have repeatedly argued that the Ministers' decision has no legal standing under the GATT treaty. The negotiations on services may be held under GATT auspices but their outcome cannot be binding on GATT members. This view that the GNS is different from the GNG has been further emphasized during the subsequent meetings of the GNS. Thus, the new GATT round was launched by separating services from goods and by avoiding the issue of whether GATT needed to be augmented in order to accommodate services.

The negotiating proposals

The negotiating agenda of the GNS, which was decided in January 1987, had initially five items. Discussions on these items of the agenda lasted throughout 1987, at the end of which there was a stock-taking session. Unlike other negotiating groups, the GNS did not have any prearranged plans on the phase of its work that was to follow in 1988. This was a reflection of the exploratory nature of the negotiations and the uncertainty as to their direction and final objectives. Between December 1987 and the mid-term review meeting in Montreal in December 1988, the GNS met to discuss proposals on the nature of a possible agreement and the principles that it might incorporate.

The initial five items were the following:

(*a*) *'Definitional and statistical issues'*. Statistics on services are imprecise. There is disagreement on how the low quality of statistics could affect the course of the negotiations. One view is that a major improvement of statistics is not a prerequisite to the successful conclusion of the negotiations. An opposite view is that GATT parties need to have a clear idea of what they concede and what they gain. Developing countries have suggested that the collection of statistics would be improved by international cooperation and technical assistance to developing countries.

The Ministerial Declaration makes mention of 'trade in services'. This is interpreted by developing countries to refer to cross-border services (e.g. flows of computer data). There is no consensus on the concepts of services and traded services, or whether they include the movement of service-providers. Movement of people and capital comes close to foreign direct investment, which, developing countries argue, is not in the remit of the Uruguay round. Moreover, developing countries maintain that if movement of service-providers is ever negotiated, it must also include movement of labour.

(*b*) *'Broad concepts on which principles and rules for trade in services, including possible disciplines for individual sectors, might be based'*. The developed-country position, as exemplified by the EC and US proposals (which are summarized in Figure 6.1), is in favour of a broad, legally binding framework that encompasses both cross-border services and services that require establishment. This position emphasizes non-discrimination, national treatment, transparency, dispute settlement and agreed codes of conduct relating to state monopolies and subsidies. The US proposal also emphasizes the right of establishment. In addition, the EC has put forth the concept of 'appropriate' regulation. Different national regulations would be permitted as long as they are deemed appropriate. A major difference between the European and the American proposals is the treatment of third countries. The US favours conditional MFN treatment, while the EC supports unconditional treatment.

The developing-country position rejects the view that GATT principles could be extended to services. It argues that GATT principles apply to goods, and that therefore there can be no national treatment of providers of services. It also rejects the idea of defining appropriate regulations. According to the Ministerial Declaration, national policies must be respected. This is interpreted by developing countries to imply that national regulations are not subject to negotiation or other international review. Some negotiators also question the validity and applicability of national treatment, transparency and non-discrimination. They are not convinced that such concepts make any contribution towards development and growth. They argue that there is a need for new concepts and principles which can directly facilitate development. Consequently, they have suggested that provisions which extend special treatment to developing countries and support their development efforts should be an integral part of an eventual agreement on services. Such provisions, they argue, should not be regarded as exceptions which are appended to a framework of distinct rules and principles. They also want new principles that define safeguard measures, exceptions and derogations relating to infant industries, strategic industries and areas of national and cultural identity.

(c) *'Coverage of the multilateral framework for trade in services'.* Developed countries have not expressed preference for any particular service sector. In principle, all services are subject to negotiation. Developing countries have been anxious to clarify that the national importance of certain sectors, such as banking, precludes them from being opened up to foreign competition. Moreover, they want the GNS to consider specifically labour-intensive services. Should factor movements be included in the negotiations, they expect that temporary labour movements will also be examined.

(*d*) *'Existing international disciplines and arrangements'*. There exist several international organizations which provide disciplines and other arrangements on the conduct and practices in specific service sectors. They may also have provisions on the treatment of service-providers. There are as yet no suggestions on how to draw on existing arrangements, such as those of aviation, maritime transportation and telecommunications.

(*e*) *'Measures and practices contributing to or limiting the expansion of trade in services, including specifically any barriers perceived by individual participants, to which the conditions of transparency and progressive liberalization might be applicable'*. The distinction between trade-related and investment-related services has divided opinion on what constitutes a barrier. For example, the US Trade Act 1988 defines restrictions to investment as barriers to trade in services. Developed countries have adopted a broad view, which includes regulations on tax treatment, competition, intellectual property rights, access to labour markets, access to foreign exchange and public procurement. The developing-country view is narrower. It focuses on cross-border services and excludes those measures which are intended to 'strengthen' the domestic service sectors.

At the GNS meetings during 1987 and 1988, several countries submitted papers elaborating the five items and suggesting the elements to be included in a possible agreement of services. Initially the discussions concentrated on the nature of service statistics and whether better data were necessary before substantive negotiations could begin. Many of the participants argued that services are essential to economic growth, and that therefore any negotiated liberalization should seek to improve the contribution of services to development. Experts from the statistical offices of the IMF, UN, UNCTAD and UNCTC made presentations outlining their own work and the scope and nature of the data they collect. There was broad consensus that developing countries would need material and technical assistance in improving their statistical services.

Most of the submissions on principles have been made by developed countries; developing countries have in general remained hostile towards the negotiations. Nevertheless, by the time of the mid-term review meeting in Montreal in December 1988, some developing countries adopted a more compromising position and

Figure 6.1 Proposals for liberalization of services

EC	USA	ARGENTINA
Objectives		
Expand trade in services Liberalize market access Standstill in protectionism Promote growth and development	Liberalize services Improve market access Standstill in protectionism Promote development and competition	Promote development (economic growth, greater participation in trade, capability adapt to new circumstances)
Coverage/Scope		
All traded services	Cross-border movement of services Establishment of foreign subsidiaries	Services that fit the definition of trade or transaction in services
Concepts/Principles		
Respect for domestic policies Unconditional MFN treatment National treatment (non- discrimination) Appropriate regulation/ liberalization: —effective market access —comparable market access —similar market opportunity	Respect for domestic policies Conditional MFN treatment National treatment (non- discrimination): —market access —no enforced establishment	Respect for domestic policies Equality of opportunity of market access Rules must be more flexible for LDCs —must be allowed to regulate services relating to development —must be allowed measures to expand exports —must be allowed to be selective in opening up domestic market —must be allowed to regulate capital flows Developed countries expand imports from LDCs Measures for technology transfer access to technology Relaxation of intellectual property rights, export controls of technology
Rules and restrictions on: —state monopolies, dominant firms —public procurement —fair competition Improved transparency Strengthened dispute settlement Escape clauses, exceptions	Rules and restrictions on: —state monopolies —accreditation —subsidies Improved transparency Strengthened dispute settlement Exceptions: —national security —measures for regulatory differences —countervailing measures	Rules on conduct and business practices of MNCs Transparency Dispute settlement
Negotiating procedure		
Permanent regulations committee Notification of perceived barriers Notification of perceived appropriate regulation Balance of rights, obligations, benefits		Executive committee Balance of rights and obligations exceptions Gradual adjustment of national rules Facilitating special agreements among LDCs

were willing to discuss a framework agreement. Brazil and India have maintained their hard-line position by insisting on the legal separation of services from the rest of the round and GATT. Other countries have requested that labour and labour-intensive services be included in the deliberations of the GNS. Some countries, however, have made counter-proposals and have sought to respond to the issues raised by developed countries. Mexico and Argentina have argued that an agreement on services has to help developing countries gain access to service markets and facilitate transfer of technology to poor countries. Yet, in their opinion, the GNS has no mandate in defining rights of establishment. A paper by Jamaica has reviewed the current state of the debate and suggested that as part of its future work the GNS should undertake studies evaluating the costs and benefits of liberalization.

The most extensive and promising paper by a developing country has been that submitted by Argentina. Its main provisions are summarized in Figure 6.1. It accepts that there could be a negotiated framework agreement in services. It stresses, however, that developing countries should be bound by such a framework only to the extent that their objectives for growth and development are not compromised: that is, they should be allowed to resort to measures that promote those objectives even if such measures restrict trade. At the mid-term review meeting in Montreal, Ministers reiterated that a service agreement ought to take into account the special needs of developing countries. They have not, however, explained what those needs might be or how they might be addressed.

Most of the papers submitted by developed countries have sought to define the principles and disciplines that would have to be incorporated in an agreement. In particular there has been analysis of the nature of non-discrimination, transparency, national treatment and regulation. The most comprehensive papers have been submitted by the US and the EC. Their main provisions are summarized in Figure 6.1. The US paper proposes a general framework of principles which would ensure unimpeded cross-border trade and movement of service-providers. Unimpeded trade is thought to require the elimination of discriminatory measures relating to treatment and establishment of service-providers. The paper suggests that the benefits from liberalization would be extended only to signatory parties (i.e. conditional most-favoured-nation treatment). It accepts that countries have a sovereign right in regulating services, but it does not elaborate on how liberalization could be reconciled with regulatory discretion. There is also reference to the need for transparency, controls on state monopolies and a mechanism for settling disputes. It is interesting to note that the paper opposes the establishment of a supranational body to review and approve domestic regulation.

In a separate submission the US has outlined a three-phase procedure for drafting and implementing a multilateral framework for trade in services. The first phase involves the negotiation of the rules and disciplines that would be incorporated in a framework. During the second phase, negotiating parties would seek to agree on a list of service industries to be covered by the general framework and by additional sectoral agreements. During this phase participants would be allowed to register their reservations with respect to existing national measures that resisted being brought into conformity with the framework agreement. Participating countries would also be allowed to enter into separate agreements with different rules on particular service sectors. The third phase would be aimed at liberalizing those measures about which signatories had previously expressed reservations.

The EC proposal reflects in general the ideas put forth by the US paper. It favours a framework of principles whose aim would be to reduce discrimination but which would do so without interfering with the national prerogative to regulate. To this extent, the paper argues for the need to define appropriate types of regulation. In contrast to the US paper, the EC proposes the establishment of a permanent committee whose responsibility would be to provide surveillance of policies on the provision of services.

At the Montreal meeting, delegates agreed that the second half of the round ought to be spent on discussing the principles that may be applicable to particular service sectors. The only principles that were unambiguously agreed upon were that service-providers should receive national treatment and that developing countries should be subject to less stringent rules than other countries.

Perceived conflicts of interest
Both economic theory and the experience of the postwar years suggest that a country is likely to benefit by engaging in trade with other countries. The perception of mutual gains is absent from the

current GATT negotiations. The source of the acrimony between developed and developing countries is the divergence of opinion on likely gains and losses. Developing countries believe that they will be net losers. Moreover, they think that the US has never really demonstrated how they may gain from liberalizing their services.

The US and other developed countries are perceived to be prompted by the following five motives:

(a) Services are increasing in prominence in most industrial economies. 'Deindustrialization' is caused partly by the shift towards more service-oriented activities. At the same time developed countries are losing their comparative advantage in low-technology manufactures. Other countries are becoming more efficient in producing simple manufactured goods.

(b) Technological advances enable more services to be traded internationally. More extensive trade could give rise to economies of scale which may allow a few firms to achieve a dominant share of the market.

(c) Unilateral domestic deregulation has increased foreign competition. Foreign markets have become by comparison more restrictive. Private companies complain of unequal treatment, which creates the impression that one objective of the developed-country policy on services is to reduce these complaints by forcing foreign governments to open up their markets. The impression that private companies exert an undue influence is reinforced by the fact that, in the case of the US, the Trade Representative has to consult private-sector committees, two of which are the Services Policy Advisory Committee (SPAC) and the joint Trade Representative-Commerce Department Industry Sector Advisory Committee on services (ISAC).

In the US there is also the Coalition of Service Industries (CSI), which is active in promoting the interests of its members. In the UK there is the British Invisibles Exports Council (BIEC) with its Liberalization of Trade in Services Committee (LOTIS). In the EC there is the European Community Services Group (ECSG), which is an umbrella organization representing service industries from the twelve members of the Community.

Not all developed-country groups, however have the same views. John Carroll, Executive Vice-President of the Communications Workers of America, has publicly spoken in favour of 'the rights of governments to enact policies which protect a broader public interest ... it is a disservice to the public interest to use the code words of "barriers to trade in services" to fight for the foreign interests of a handful of large construction, banking and insurance firms'.[3]

(d) Liberalization of trade in services is thought to complement other policy goals that relate to trade in high-technology products, intellectual property rights and foreign direct investment. These issues, which are new to GATT, are considered to be part of the 'grand trade-off' (Bhagwati, 1987) in the US trade strategy. In return for the expected benefits from these new sectors, the US is willing to undertake rollbacks and standstills on goods. The US also believes that GATT is increasingly outmoded and superseded by changes in the international economy. Thus, GATT is in need of general overhaul to incorporate the new type of economic transactions.

(e) Protectionist feeling is fuelled by the perception that other countries have failed to reciprocate to the more liberal policies of western countries. The US position on services is also determined by the more general shift in trade policy which seeks greater reciprocity and more symmetrical obligations from its trade partners (Bhagwati, 1987).

Initially the EC had doubts about the US initiative on services. Its position, however, has gradually changed. In the course of the efforts to integrate its internal market it has discovered that the Community is the largest exporter of services such as transportation and travel. In these services it exports more than three times as much as either the US or Japan. Moreover, the EC has increased its support of the US because of its unilateral internal liberalization. It fears that, in the absence of reciprocal changes by other countries, foreign firms may benefit more than EC firms from the dismantling of the internal barriers (Kakabadse, 1987, p. 58).

Japan has emerged as the strongest ally of the US on the issue of services. Japan has not been a prominent exporter of services. This situation, however, is changing rapidly. In the sectors of transportation and travel Japan has a large deficit. By contrast, in financial services Japanese institutions are gaining worldwide prominence. For example, in 1971 the three largest banks in the world (ranked by size of deposits) were American: Bank of America, First National City Bank and Chase Manhattan Bank. In 1986, the three largest were Japanese: Dai Ichi Kangyo Bank, Fuji Bank and Sumitomo Bank.[4]

Japan supports the liberal position of the US because it sees the possibility not only of commercial gains but also of political gains. It wants to deflect some of the criticism about its trade surplus and closed market by showing a more liberal stance. It is under pressure to liberalize and deregulate its domestic market, and it therefore wants to gain similar access to foreign markets (Kakabadse, 1987, p. 60).

Developing countries object to GATT-sponsored negotiations on services because they believe that liberalization will primarily benefit industrial countries. However, some of them (e.g. Argentina) are in favour of some kind of agreement that would safeguard their rights and would impose a code of conduct on service-suppliers. The hardliners among them (i.e. Brazil, Cuba, Egypt, India, Nicaragua, Nigeria, Peru and Tanzania) dispute the legality of the negotiations on services. The main features of their position, which are presented below, have been gathered from statements made by their negotiators during the 1987–8 meetings of the GNS and the November 1987 meeting of the North-South Roundtable. They are a diverse group and what is presented as a collective view has been influenced by the more vocal countries among them. They oppose GATT negotiations for several reasons:

(a) GATT is perceived to be an organization where countries negotiate by accepting legal obligations and binding commitments. This is seen as being in favour of the US plan for a general framework of disciplines on trade in services. Developing countries would prefer a sectoral approach, whereby each service industry would be examined separately according to its possible impact on their development and growth. They do not want to be constrained by a legal structure, because they think that loss of policy autonomy will be disadvantageous to 'weak' countries such as themselves. They would emphasize, instead, safeguards, exclusions and exceptions rather than general and binding principles. The only principle they would accept is the need to promote development. They would prefer a framework that enhances the 'stability' and 'predictability', rather than the openness, of the trading system (Helleiner, 1987; North-South Roundtable, 1987).

(b) GATT is a liberal organization, which is again seen as being favourable to the US objective of opening up markets. Brazil and India have repeatedly emphasized that the Ministerial Declaration stated that liberalization was a means to economic growth and development. They do not think, therefore, that the GATT framework is either suitable or conducive to discussions on development strategies. They consider other fora, such as UNCTAD and UNIDO, to be more receptive to their needs. Organizations such as the UNCTC are also regarded as being more appropriate because they deal with multinational companies (MNCs), which are thought to be the major international providers of services. Stalson (1985) observes that other fora have tended to manage trade rather than liberalize it. Trade management and active regulation of market forces are more akin to the ideological predilections of many developing countries.

Developing countries argue that the GATT custom of negotiated concessions is incompatible with the commitment in the Uruguay Declaration to respect national policies. Since national policies are not subject to negotiation, there is nothing to be conceded away. They are apprehensive that multilateral negotiations on the right of establishment will prove to be the Trojan horse for circumventing national controls on foreign investment.

(c) At the launching of the Uruguay round the developing countries insisted on a twin-track process that separated services from goods. They did so in order that their manufacturing products should gain greater access to the markets of developed countries. Moreover, the fact that there is no standstill or rollback provision in services is a strong indication that industrial countries may attempt to link concessions in goods to concessions in services.

They argue that GATT should complete the dismantling of barriers on the trade of goods before it extends its scope into new issues. They point out that there is virtual lack of progress on issues which are of particular interest to them, such as the Multi-Fibre Arrangement (MFA) and the Generalized System of Preferences (GSP). Services are seen as distracting from the urgency of solving those problems.

(d) Developing countries have also claimed that it is premature to initiate multilateral negotiations on services. They maintain that they are not adequately prepared to participate in substantive negotiations on specific service sectors and business practices. Data on services are incomplete and highly aggregated. Moreover, there is sketchy understanding of the volume and nature of transactions that take place within MNCs.

In summary, they oppose the inclusion of services in GATT partly because they think GATT has other more important responsibilities and partly because GATT is not yet considered a suitable forum. There now arise two questions: Is GATT the right place to liberalize services? And, can GATT accommodate at the same time the special interests and needs of developing countries? The second question is considered more extensively in the following chapter. The rest of this chapter examines the nature of GATT and whether it is suitable for dealing with all the complexities of services.

The nature of GATT
The keystone of GATT is the principle of non-discrimination (Arts. I and XIII). It requires all signatory countries to extend most-favoured-nation (MFN) treatment unconditionally to all other member countries. The only distinction that can be made between domestic and foreign goods is by border measures in the form of tariffs. This implies that foreign products are entitled to national treatment once they are inside a national market (Art. III). It also implies that member countries should refrain from using non-tariff barriers.

GATT is not a free trade institution; it merely provides a forum in which interested countries can negotiate the reduction of their trade barriers. GATT, however, requires that once these barriers are reduced they are also bound. It 'favours' the use of tariffs over other trade restrictions because even though GATT is not a free trade institution, it is, nonetheless, based on liberal economic principles. Tariffs are consistent with the price mechanism, they allow adjustment to changes in competitiveness and comparative advantages, they are visible or transparent and they can be used in a non-discriminatory manner (Viravan et al., 1987, p. 26).

GATT has been weakened in recent years by measures that breach both its spirit and its letter. For extensive analyses and assessment of the state of the trading system, see Bhagwati (1988) and Viravan et al. (1987). Most disruptive among these measures are the so-called 'grey area' instruments, such as 'voluntary export restraints', 'orderly marketing arrangements' and other preferential trade agreements. These measures are opaque (non-transparent), prevent market adjustment and explicitly discriminate among products and their suppliers.

If non-discrimination, national treatment and transparency are what GATT is all about, can it accommodate services? What GATT can do is, of course, largely determined by its signatory countries. Some countries have argued that the GATT Treaty does not refer to services and would not apply to non-traded services because GATT is about trade. In response to this, it has been pointed out that many of the impediments to trade in services can be dealt with within GATT even if the treaty does not refer to them explicitly (see Balasubramanyam, 1988a, 1988b; Hindley, 1986a, 1986b, 1987). Indeed, as argued in Chapters 2 and 3, the separation between traded and non-traded services depends on available technology, not on any intrinsic or immutable characteristic of services. It appears, therefore, that there is a respectable literature that supports the suitability of GATT as a forum for liberalizing services. It would be unproductive to argue along the all-or-nothing line. As in most other disputes, this is an issue of degree, and a more productive approach would be to examine which of the characteristics or elements of GATT are suitable, which are unsuitable and whether the latter can be amended.

GATT is suitable to the extent that it encourages the negotiated reduction and binding of protectionist measures. Many of the restrictions in the provision of services simply protect domestic providers by discriminating against foreign providers (Hindley, 1988a). The view that many such measures are non-border, incorporated in national policies and, thus, beyond the scope of GATT is exceedingly legalistic. GATT does require national treatment, which in turn would require non-discriminatory treatment of foreign firms, including service-providers. Border measures are part of national economic policies, yet they have been subject to negotiation. The fact that non-border measures are part of national policies is not a convincing argument for excluding them from GATT.

The same applies to the view that movement of factors of production are outside GATT's remit. Restrictions on movement are for many services equivalent to restrictions on trade. Again, on the basis of an excessively legalistic attitude, it could be argued that GATT does not apply to movement of labour and capital. If, however, one examines the purpose and intentions of GATT, there is no reason for excluding factor movements because the liberalization of such movements directly facilitates transactions (trade) in services between residents and non-residents.

Much of the disagreement about the suitability of GATT stems from conflicting interpretations of the purpose of the GATT Treaty.

On the one side there is a 'fundamentalist' group, whose position is based on a strictly legal assessment of the scope of the treaty; on the opposite side there is a 'reformist' group, whose opinion is shaped by an interpretation of the general purpose and intentions of the treaty. They do not regard the treaty as having specified any explicit limits as to the areas and aspects of international economic exchange that it applies to. Because the treaty is seen as having the general purpose of facilitating trade, the reformists consider appropriate and desirable the inclusion of any new measure that is found to obstruct trade. Hence, the fundamentalists rely on a definition of measures, whereas the reformists rely on a definition of effects.

The fundamentalist position is untenable in that GATT has been evolving ever since its inception in 1949. The evolution and augmentation of GATT has been guided by a broad understanding of its purpose. Hence, there is much merit and precedence supporting the reformist view on services. Now, given that a consensus is reached on the need to expand trade in services, can GATT cope both as an institution and as a set of rules with the special problems of services?

The problem which is likely to cause much difficulty is that of regulation. Because many services are subject to regulatory supervision and because regulatory standards vary, there may be good economic reasons for imposing measures that restrict trade and/or the movement of service-providers. Of course, this argument does not imply that all restrictions can be justified. Nor does it prove the logical necessity of trade measures. Regulatory differences need not always justify restrictive measures. The argument merely indicates the logical possibility of such measures. Therefore, whether a measure is discriminatory depends both on a country's regulatory regime and on whom it is targeted at. It follows that whether a country should reduce or revoke that measure depends on the regulatory standards that prevail in the country of origin of the beneficiary foreign providers. Because of the need for safeguarding regulatory integrity, it is likely that liberalization in services would have to be *selective*.

Selectivity, however, runs counter to GATT principles and it is also to a large extent against the GATT custom of reciprocal liberalization. Selectivity conflicts with the basic tenet of MFN treatment. But MFN treatment cannot be granted precisely because regulatory regimes differ. Reciprocity, meaning the removal of similar measures, or even of measures with equivalent effects, may also be difficult to achieve. Countries with different regimes are likely to use different policy measures and rules. But, even if there can be found similar measures, they need not be of equal discriminatory magnitude. Moreover, the effect of their removal largely depends on the nature of national regimes. The same measure may have serious implications in one country and negligible effects in another.

Selectivity may also be a component of efficient regulatory supervision. Because supervision may need to react to changing conditions in the world economy and in particular countries, the treatment of both domestic and foreign firms may have to be both selective and non-transparent in the sense that regulatory authorities would retain a degree of discretion in adjusting regulatory requirements. Thus, as long as there are regulatory differences, cross-border trade in services may necessitate policies that contravene basic GATT principles and could undermine the GATT system.

There are two possible ways of avoiding the difficulties caused by regulatory differences. The first is more ambitious than current proposals and it is similar to the EC's approach to liberalization. In addition to a reduction of entry barriers, it would involve a minimum but necessary degree of harmonization. However, it is unlikely that this will happen at GATT because of the sheer immensity of the task of getting 96 countries to agree to harmonize their regulations. Perhaps they should not harmonize them, since it would be equally difficult to adjust them subsequently in response to changing economic conditions.

The second approach is more circumspect than current proposals. It would require that signatory parties extend national treatment to all firms operating in their national markets irrespective of their origin. This simple rule would not force any country to change its regulatory system. Each country would still be allowed to exercise control over who enters its markets by using entry restrictions at the border, as GATT stipulates. Instead of refusing establishment, they could require establishment as a precondition to provision of services. As discussed in the following chapter, this is an attractive alternative for developing countries. A GATT committee could be established to assess whether that treatment is indeed non-discriminatory. Other safeguards, obligations and a dispute settlement procedure could also be agreed upon. At the same time there could be negotiations for the reduction of those border restrictions that are found to be purely discriminatory without any regulatory function. GATT should not prevent groups of countries from negotiating regulatory harmonization that would facilitate cross-border trade. In a recent study on a constitutional framework for services, Professor John Jackson (1988) has proposed a multi-tiered agreement with different levels of obligations and benefits. In this way a country would have the option to join the agreement at the level which it thinks it suits its economic circumstances. A multi-tiered agreement would allow different groups of countries to liberalize more extensively without having to include less enthusiastic GATT members.

Professor Jackson also proposes that the process of liberalization could begin with the establishment of a permanent secretariat-type institution, whose purpose would be to facilitate continual consultation and negotiation on new service sectors or new problems that were not previously considered. As noted in Chapter 4, it is important to have a permanent institution continually reviewing national policies because, as long as countries maintain regulatory autonomy, liberalization would be an ongoing process.

Professor Jackson's reason for proposing that an institution be established first is that GATT members, in his view, are not yet willing to make any major commitments, such as granting national treatment. A major theme in this paper is that if liberalization is to be irreversible, it is essential that participating countries undertake substantial commitments which would also include accepting international review of their policies. If indeed GATT can proceed only in a gradual and piecemeal fashion, then one can only hope that there is no major disturbance in the world economy which countries could use as an excuse to disown their commitments.

Conclusion

There seem to be no economic reasons for excluding all aspects of services from GATT disciplines. The opposing (mostly developing) countries, motivated by non-economic concerns, have developed a legalistic position to defend their objection to the liberalization of services. Proponents may have overlooked, however, the complexity of services and their regulations. Because differences in regulatory standards may be transmitted by cross-border trade, liberalization of that trade may not be an optimum policy. An alternative approach could initially involve the undertaking of the obligation to extend national treatment to all locally established service-providers. This simple rule, however, would diverge from the GATT custom of reciprocal concessions, since some countries would have to eliminate more restrictive measures than others.

Notes

1 'Yeutter Hits Blockers of Trade Talks', *Washington Post*, 15 November 1985, p. 25.
2 'Trade Aides Fail to Narrow Differences Prior to the New Round of GATT Talks', *Wall Street Journal*, 8 September 1986, p. 3.
3 Quoted in Stalson, 1985, p. vii.
4 *International Economy*, January/February 1988, vol. 2, p. 25.

7
ACCOMMODATING DEVELOPING COUNTRIES

The preceding chapter reviewed the state of the GATT negotiations and the various proposals that have been submitted at the GNS. It was argued that liberalization of services requires a departure from the GATT tradition of exchanging reciprocal and equivalent concessions. Instead, there should be rules on the treatment of foreign service-providers.

The developing countries which oppose the introduction of services into GATT reject even more resolutely the idea that trade policy and national regulations should be bound by internationally agreed rules. The chapter examines the position of the developing countries on this issue and their concerns about loss of autonomy in policy-making. It also assesses their demands for special and differential treatment to promote their development and competitiveness in the world markets for services.

Preferential treatment of developing countries has always been fraught with problems. It is argued in this chapter that the case for preferential treatment in services is even more tenuous. By contrast, the case for general and non-preferential rules is reinforced further when considering that services are invisibles, which may need to be regulated, and that some of them can only be delivered personally by their providers.

Developing countries should be in favour of a rules-based agreement not only because rules make economic sense but mostly because it is in their interests to do so. Because governments could easily use regulation as a pretext for discrimination and because preferential treatment leaves too much potentially abusable discretion in trade policy-making, developing countries would be better-off in the long run if they chose instead to accept obligations on a contractually equal basis with other countries. Binding rules should compensate for their lack of economic might. The following section examines the reasons why developing countries should not be alarmed by the prospect of liberalization and reduction in their discretion to discriminate in favour of their domestic service industries.

It should be clarified at this point that even though most developing countries share the same view on services, there are variations among them. A few, rapidly growing, developing countries, such as Singapore, actually welcome the prospect of trade liberalization. But the majority of them have hardly participated in the negotiations. What has become the 'developing country position' is largely shaped by the arguments of the most vocal opponents of the GATT talks.

Developing country concerns

Developing countries have often argued that liberal trade policy is detrimental to their growth and development. They have been reluctant to accept GATT disciplines and their position in GATT has been one of taking exception to the obligations required of other members on the grounds that they should be accorded 'special and differential' treatment (Riedel, 1987; Hudec, 1988). It is not surprising, therefore, that most of them have not supported the idea of liberalizing services, while some of them have actively opposed it.

Their opposition to service negotiations has been motivated by a number of additional concerns about the impact of liberalization on their economies and about their ability to compete in international markets for services. The purpose of this section is to examine these concerns and argue that liberalization need not be detrimental. It might have some negative effects, but they need not be either the only or the dominant effects. Thus, this section presents an alternative perspective or scenario which so far has not been considered by developing countries. In particular they have raised the following issues:

(a) Effects of liberalization

It is difficult to predict the effects of opening up trade in services because statistics are inaccurate, and because there is as yet no generally accepted theory on how countries produce and trade services. Because trade may require movement of providers, it is thought that the traditional theory of comparative advantage does not apply to services. Whether this view is correct is largely irrelevant to the issue of liberalization. Developing countries should consider instead whether liberalization would be of net benefit to them rather than try to predict the pattern of world trade in services. The opening up of domestic markets may put competitive pressure on local service firms, but there are several reasons why this need not be detrimental to the economy of a developing country.

The availability of cheaper services would improve the efficiency of the domestic economy. The users of newly available producer services would be able either to expand their output and raise its quality, or to make its distribution and marketing more effective. Since producer services increase the value-added in production, exports would consequently become more competitive. Liberalization, therefore, need not worsen the balance of payments, since in the long run imported services would help domestic producers to expand their exports. Not only are imported services likely to be cheaper, but they are even more likely to be of higher quality and, thus, of greater benefit to their users. For example, a statistical study by Tucker and Sundberg (1986) has found a positive relationship between exports and the amount of services which are used as inputs (measured in terms of value).

Imports of those services whose provision requires the presence of the providers may put competitive pressure on domestic firms but it need not raise unemployment. On the contrary, it is more likely to reduce unemployment since newly established firms would have to hire some local personnel. If local employees underwent training, the domestic economy would derive an additional benefit from a transfer of skills of the foreign service firms. Balasubramanyam (1988b) observes that foreign firms may be able to provide their services more easily through the medium of direct investment because ownership of the local subsidiary may be the most efficient method for transferring skills, firm-specific assets and other proprietary information. Again, this transfer of skills which are necessary for the provision of competitive services also improves the export performance of both manufacturing and services of the host economy. Balasubramanyam describes this skill-transferring type of investment as 'trade-enhancing' because it strengthens a country's comparative advantage and contributes to its export potential.

The apprehension of developing countries that liberalization may facilitate the domination of their economies by multinational companies is to some extent justified. However, it does not necessarily follow that the appropriate policy response to this problem is the outright exclusion of foreign companies from their domestic markets. As Riedel (1987, pp. 87–91) notes, policies which are aimed at reducing dependency often succeed in increasing it. For example, selective licensing of foreign companies may in fact accentuate non-competitive practices and pricing because it prevents potential competitors from offering their services. Avoiding exploitation by MNCs may instead be more successfully achieved by a combination of anti-trust policy and more liberal disposition towards foreign firms that provide the competitive counterbalance to the firms that already operate in the domestic market.

(b) Competing in world markets

Several statistical studies have supported the conventional view that it is the industrial countries that have the comparative advantage in the production and trade of services (e.g. Sapir and Lutz, 1980, 1981). These studies, however, have examined the data only on those services that are recorded in balance-of-payments statistics (e.g. shipping, transportation, travel). Peterson and Barras (1987) have argued that if the volume of trade is adjusted by the size of a country's economy, then certain developing countries can also be shown to have a comparative advantage in those services. Nevertheless, there is a widespread belief among developing country negotiators that MNCs are the only service-providers that can survive the cut-throat competition of world markets. They are perceived as having the necessary skills, experience, technology, operating economies of scale, distribution networks, image, reputation and client loyalty. While all these characteristics may correctly describe service MNCs, it can also be argued that for many services cheap and well-trained labour is the major factor contributing to competitiveness: e.g. Korean construction workers, Filipino ship crews, Singaporean air stewardesses.

However, this debate of where comparative advantage lies misses the point. Why are developing countries interested now in becoming competitive in services? So far they have not been exporting any significant amount of services, so why has export performance become an obstacle preventing liberalization? The root of the problem is the old issue of infant industries. Liberalization is thought to stunt the growth of nascent service industries. But can protection and isolation from world markets contribute to industrial growth? How can entrepreneurship thrive in an environment of constant bureaucratic intervention? In a recent study on the effect of inward investment in several European countries, Sharp (1988) has found that the indigenous industries which have experienced marked improvement in their market position are those which had entered into joint and other cooperative ventures with foreign investors. These ventures have facilitated the acquisition of skills, and of technological and market knowledge, by the local partners. Joint ventures and market contact would be even more important in services where skills and knowledge are embodied in their providers. Sharp has also found that over the medium term managers who get trained by the foreign investors and then move to local firms also improve the competitiveness of those firms. Thus, in addition to theory, there is considerable empirical evidence that blanket protectionism is not conducive to the growth of infant industries.

(c) Loss of national economic autonomy
It is feared that liberalization would result in a loss of national economic autonomy. For some services, liberalization would be equivalent to allowing the establishment of foreign firms in the domestic market. In this sense a country would forgo control over which firm is allowed to enter its market. But it could still maintain its policies regarding the operations of any firm within its jurisdiction. It should be realized, however, that policy autonomy, like most other economic issues, is a matter of degree. Even if links with the world economy are severed, policy autonomy need not improve whenever the options available to the policy-makers are also curtailed.

Liberalization of trade in services inevitably raises the issue of investment because certain services can be provided only by the establishment of the service-provider in the domestic market. Developing countries have contended that investment is not a trade issue, and that therefore it is not subject to negotiation. This is an overly legalistic attitude. Establishment may be the only way by which some services can be delivered. Whether that is legally classified as investment is irrelevant to the issue of liberalizing transactions in services between foreign providers and domestic clients. What matters is not the legal classification but the effect of liberalizing establishment.

A government that becomes party to an agreement which provides for international disciplines on services would indeed forgo some of its discretion in discriminating arbitrarily against foreign providers. But at the same time it gains the right to expect similar treatment from the other members of the agreement. Perceiving an agreement on services only as a loss of national policy autonomy is misleadingly incomplete. Such an agreement should be more accurately regarded as an exchange of the prerogative to expect particular treatment by foreign governments.

It ought to be acknowledged, however, that certain services, such as advertising and film distribution, may generate ideas and present images which may be thought offensive to the culture of certain developing countries. The issue which arises is often described as a conflict between liberalism/secularism and traditionalism. Although this issue may be important to certain societies, it by no means characterizes the majority of services, which are free from these conflicting cultural elements. Protection of cultural heritage should not be an excuse for the protection of transportation, accounting, banking, engineering, computer programming, etc.

(d) Negotiating linkages

An objection of developing countries to the inclusion of services in the Uruguay round has been that services would distract the negotiators' efforts and slow down progress on other issues. Developing countries are also suspicious of the inclusion of services because concessions on manufacturing and agricultural goods by industrial countries may be implicitly tied to concessions on services by developing countries. It is probably true that an agenda of too many items would induce negotiating fatigue. Nonetheless, it may also facilitate the process of reaching a balance of concessions since a large agenda could increase the possible number of compromising trade-offs.

The crucial question is not whether services should have been included, but what would happen should developing countries withdraw from the negotiations and what the effects of non-participation would be. Irrespective of whether it is right or wrong, the likely immediate effect would be a reinforcing of the negotiating link between services and goods. But, even if this did not happen, non-participation of developing countries would have other negative effects that would become increasingly obvious in the long term. It is unlikely that withdrawal of developing countries would stop industrial countries from concluding an agreement outside GATT. Jackson (1988) observes that if a group of countries conclude an agreement among themselves in order to avoid the 'foot-dragging' of other, less enthusiastic, GATT members, they should make their concessions conditional upon membership of the agreement. Non-members would not be able to 'free-ride' and share the benefits from liberalization. The precedent set by the Tokyo round codes entails that a code-type agreement on services would afford MFN treatment only to the member countries.

A potentially more detrimental ramification of non-participation is not that developing countries will reap none of the benefits but that the agreed rules and other disciplines could positively discriminate against their interests. For example, industrial countries are not likely to implement rules on the movement of labour or on labour-intensive, low-skill services. Developing countries would be able to influence the scope of the agreement only by participating in the negotiations.

Moreover, non-participation does not mean that they would not have to reconsider whether to open up their protected markets. They would still be vulnerable to bilateral pressure. Membership of an agreement which provides for specified stages of liberalization would enable them to use their contractual rights to fend off pressure from economically more powerful countries. And they would also be able to launch a complaint should other countries attempt to blackmail them by discriminating against them. An agreement would give them rights as well as obligations in a trading world in which they lack economic might.

Developing countries will face increasing pressure both from other countries and from their own industries to relax their restrictions on the trade of services. It would be unwise of them to withdraw from the current negotiations and miss the opportunity of shaping the nascent international rules on the trade of services. The following section examines what rules developing countries should pursue and what kind of an agreement they should want to draft.

Rules for developing countries

Should an agreement accommodate developing country demands, such as those tabled by Argentina at the GNS (see Figure 6.1)? The answer depends on whether the aim is to conclude, seemingly successfully, the Uruguay round or to implement rules that would facilitate trade and reduce the likelihood of recurrent commercial disputes. Some of the demands by developing countries would exacerbate trade relations because they could make the trade system both inflexible and arbitrary.

The system would become inflexible as a result of granting preferential treatment to developing countries. Experience with the Generalized System of Preferences has shown that trade preferences actually impose constraints on the growth of exports of those countries whose industries are the most competitive (Langhammer and Sapir, 1987). Moreover, discrimination and bureaucratic discretion are inherent in the concept of preferences (Nicolaides, 1988). The reason is that preferences are accompanied by qualifications and rules determining which countries are eligible recipients. Donor countries retain the discretion to change arbitrarily those qualifications.

Developing countries have suggested that an agreement on services should incorporate the right to preferential treatment so as to reduce the discretion exercised by the trade officials of donor countries. But preferential export quotas or market shares codified in a treaty would dislocate the functioning of the market as a mechanism of allocating resources and would freeze trade in its existing pattern. Moreover, what form should preferences take in services? Disembodied services which can be traded across borders (e.g. computer programmes) are not normally stopped at the border for customs valuation purposes. Preferential treatment may take the form of favourable tax treatment, but then it would be exceedingly difficult for the tax authorities to establish the true national origin of such services. Should preferences, therefore, target only embodied services in the form of quotas on the number of foreign service-providers that are allowed to establish commercial presence in the domestic market? Because services are intangible, the task of designing trade preferences which are not based on a quota system is both difficult and elusive, since service-providers could easily circumvent any restrictions. By contrast, a system of quotas would be very distortionary, since it would prevent competition and growth of service markets.

Another suggestion by developing countries (which is also an item in Argentina's proposal) is that the host developing country should have the right to determine unilaterally when to open its market and whom to admit. This is another aspect of 'special and differential' treatment whereby developing countries do not have to reciprocate to other countries' liberalization. But this kind of discretionary policy would introduce more arbitrariness in the system and would increase uncertainty about market access. Service-providers in industrial countries would complain of unfair treatment and would put pressure on their governments to retaliate. Developing country governments would also be the target of protectionist pressure from those of their own national firms that stand to lose out from liberalization. An agreement that does not put an end to this kind of pressure is not an agreement that is likely to survive the vicissitudes of trade. Viravan et al. (1987) identify as one of the constitutional functions of international treaties the protection of governments and policy-makers from insidious domestic lobbying.

In the long term, therefore, developing countries would benefit more from an agreement that provides for well-defined rights and obligations on equal footing with other more developed countries. They should become members of the agreement whenever their economies are ready; but, when they do so, they should make a firm commitment to liberalization as contractually equal partners. It is in their interests that an eventual GATT agreement should have sectoral-based codes so that they would have the option to open up their economies sequentially and sector by sector, according to where they perceive their competitive strength to be. They may also be given the option of a longer transitional period when they join the agreement. Feketekuty (1988) provides an extensive analysis of the various sectoral agreements that may be included in a framework agreement.

Professor Jackson (1988), in his recently proposed constitutional framework for services, suggests that many developed countries would also have difficulty signing an agreement with extensive obligations that apply to all services. As already noted, he proposes the establishment of a 'multi-tiered' institution, with several levels of benefits and obligations; a country would then have the option to join the agreement at the level at which obligations are acceptable to it. Even in this more modest and pragmatic proposal, benefits are commensurate with obligations. Thus, developing countries need not again exempt themselves from international obligations. They could join gradually as their economies learn to adjust to international competition.

It seems, however, that developing countries are determined to seek exceptions for themselves. At the Montreal meeting in December 1988, they showed more willingness to accept a GATT agreement on services, provided that they would not have to undertake reciprocal obligations. Indeed, one of the very few unequivocal elements of the Ministerial Communiqué (which, however, was not adopted as a result of wrangling on agricultural and other issues) was that developing countries would be allowed to maintain or reimpose restrictive trade measures 'in line with their development situation'. It remains to be seen how other countries treat those developing countries that retain their protectionist policies as a means of promoting economic growth.

Conclusion

Developing countries are understandably worried about the impact of liberalization, not only because it would open up trade, but also because it would bring a degree of deregulation to some of the traditionally most heavily regulated industries. Services are vital in every sector of growing and increasingly specializing economies. It would be difficult for poor countries to accelerate their development process without allowing their domestic industry to have access to the international markets for services.

Asking for preferential treatment is tempting but dangerous. Such treatment can easily be entangled in a mass of rules specifying eligibility and the nature of permissible service activities. In the long run, developing countries are likely to benefit more by a non-discriminatory trade regime that enables them to use their potential economic dynamism and offers them opportunities for growth.

8
PROSPECTS FOR SUCCESS

This paper has examined what the special characteristics of services imply for trade policy. The main conclusion which emerges is that foreign service-providers should be treated in the same manner as domestic providers. The objective of consumer protection does not justify measures that discriminate against foreign providers on any grounds other than their competence to perform high-quality services. Nor will discrimination be eliminated if trade barriers are reduced on the basis of some 'equivalent reciprocity'. The pursuit of equivalent reciprocity will not lead to equal treatment of all service-providers in a market.

It is perhaps appropriate in this last chapter to turn the analysis from descriptive to predictive and examine the prospects for further liberalization of trade in services. In particular, policy-makers need to become aware of those factors that may cause the process of liberalization to falter and lead to a revival of protectionism.

Obstacles to trade liberalization
The deregulation of domestic services and the reduction of trade barriers should be seen within the broader context of what has been called the 'conservative revolution' – the shift to more market-oriented policies. Some trade barriers have been eliminated unilaterally by countries attempting to increase market competition, efficiency and service quality. For example, deregulation of financial markets in the US, Britain and Australia has been motivated by the

belief that less-regulated markets can produce superior results to more tightly controlled markets.

Instances of unilateral liberalization have received less publicity than the EC's 1992 project and GATT's negotiations because liberalization has usually been only part of a general policy reform whose primary aim was the elimination of domestic uncompetitive practices. Nevertheless, in markets where trade is controlled by bilateral arrangements, such as air transportation, domestic deregulation has had no direct effect on international trade. Deregulation of civil aviation in the US, for example, has not in itself improved the market access of foreign airlines.

Liberalization has been facilitated by a shift towards more conservative economic policy. It is more likely to be sustained if the major trading countries maintain their belief in the efficiency of the market system and the benefits of open trade. Political parties which support more interventionist domestic policies have also been in favour of more interventionist trade policies. It is unlikely that a change in the domestic political sentiment towards the left will leave external policies unaffected. An important reason why a multilateral agreement on services should be binding is that it can be less vulnerable to the vicissitudes of domestic policies.

It should be realized that conservative economic policy has not always meant more liberal trade policy. The Reagan administration pursued a policy which was more concerned with the fairness of other countries' trade measures. The Trade Act of 1988 requires the President to take whatever action is necessary to achieve the reduction of foreign unfair practices and other measures that obstruct access of American companies to foreign markets. The Trade Act is motivated by the idea that other countries should offer benefits reciprocal to those available to foreign companies in the US. The issue of reciprocity has also acquired prominence in the EC's plans on the integration of its internal financial markets. As explained in Chapter 4, in certain cases where services are regulated, trade may be liberalized only on a reciprocal basis. It is quite possible that trade officials would attempt to augment the scope and applicability of reciprocity so that it becomes a major feature of any bilateral or multilateral agreement on services. Indeed, during the mid-term review session of the Uruguay round in Montreal, in December 1988, the EC attempted to introduce into the negotiating process some of its own understanding of reciprocity.

Reciprocity is in essence a method of liberalization which is not much different from bilateral disarmament. I disarm (liberalize) when you disarm (liberalize). Therefore reciprocal liberalization should eventually lead to a barrier-free trading world. There are, however, indications that reciprocity has been interpreted in ways which are not compatible with a process leading to free trade. In particular, the EC's 1992 project has caused concern among the Community's trade partners that they could be excluded from its planned integrated market. EC leaders meeting in Rhodes in December 1988 sought to allay those concerns by assuring other countries that 1992 is only an exercise in consolidating what was started in 1958. Despite these assurances that 1992 will not create a 'fortress Europe', there have been conflicting and confusing signals on the prospects of market access by foreign firms.

A view that has often been expressed by some Commission officials and prominent European industrialists is that the benefits from the completion of the internal market should be available only to those countries that provide comparable benefits to EC companies. The justification for seeking reciprocity is that it is a market-opening instrument which will promote rather than impede trade.

A problem in assessing the significance of reciprocity is that the draft directives on banking and financial services which have clauses on reciprocity do not define it. One interpretation of reciprocity is equivalence of the benefits of market access. A weaker version is the mutual elimination of similar restrictions. Another version is a mutual commitment to treat foreign firms in the same way as domestic firms. This last version, which is essentially the same as national treatment, would allow treatment to vary among countries with different regulatory structures. The many difficulties of implementing the various types of reciprocity, and especially equivalent reciprocity, are analysed in Chapters 4 and 6 and in Nicolaides (1989).

The essential task here is to ask the following question. If the Commission intends to use reciprocity as an instrument for furthering the cause of liberal trade, what should it do? In other words, is there anything missing in the Commission's approach that reduces the credibility of its stated intention?

Reciprocity has value mainly as a strategic trade instrument which seeks to influence the policy of other countries. But strategic behaviour invites retaliation. It is, therefore, more likely to achieve its purpose (a) if its objective is clear to target countries, (b) if, when a similar policy is implemented by another country, it leads to the same objective, and (c) if it is seen not to be capricious. Rather, it should be consistent with some principle of the international trading system which should also bind the country that initiates the strategic policy.

The EC pronouncements on reciprocity fail all three of these criteria. So far they have been ambiguous, confusing and confused. It is a sign that the Community itself is uncertain as to the meaning of reciprocity and that there are internal conflicting opinions as to the purpose of seeking reciprocity. Suppose, however, that the Community eventually agrees that access to its market by foreign firms will be contingent on reciprocal arrangements by other countries: can it presume to be able to measure equivalence of benefits in any sense other than a tally of legal/regulatory requirements? The answer is no, because it cannot know how service-providers will operate in changing markets under an evolving regulatory regime. The EC would be attempting to use an unworkable policy instrument.

Even more worrying about the pursuit of reciprocity are the consequences of the adoption of similar policies by other countries. If, for example, different countries follow a policy of free trade, then each country's policy is compatible with those of other countries. This is not so for reciprocity. By following the EC's logic, the US, for example, could claim that, because of its own less restrictive trade-union legislation, European firms in the US enjoy benefits which are not available to American firms in Europe. Or, could an improvement in telecommunications which further integrated American financial markets justify exclusion of European firms because market conditions are different in Europe? Seeking to establish equivalence of the benefits of market access can be used and abused by any country which wants to discriminate against foreign firms.

The pursuit of equivalent reciprocity is also inconsistent with the principles that the EC has espoused in its 1992 project. Each member country has accepted the obligation to extend national treatment to firms from other member countries even if its own firms receive different treatment in those countries (see Chapter 5). As noted above, extending national treatment is a weaker form of reciprocity than equivalent reciprocity. So why does the EC pursue one form of reciprocity internally and another externally? Such inconsistent behaviour does not give much assurance to other countries that the Community's motives are not protectionist.

The Commission has said that already established foreign companies would be exempted from any reciprocity test. Only newcomers would be subject to that test. But what is a newcomer? What is the status of a new subsidiary of an established bank, a subsidiary which is set up for tax reasons and for the purpose of servicing its own parent, a financial subsidiary of an established manufacturing firm or a joint venture by an EC and a foreign bank? Would takeovers by foreign banks have to obtain prior approval by the Commission? All these as yet unanswered questions indicate that in an increasingly integrated world the determination of national origin has a large element of arbitrariness.

The pursuit of any kind of reciprocity is fraught with difficulties. But it must be acknowledged that gaining entry into the service markets of many countries is severely impeded not only for European firms. Instead of equivalent benefits, the EC should demand the elimination of entry barriers and other discriminatory treatment of its firms. Hence, it should want reciprocal rights of establishment (i.e. market access) and national treatment.

Denial of access to the EC market may in the end be the only way by which other countries are persuaded to open up their own markets. But resorting to trade restrictions should be the last step in a process leading from identification of particular discriminatory practices to an attempt to negotiate them away. In the EC's pronouncements on reciprocity this process seems to be reversed. It appears that all foreign applications for establishment of commercial presence within the Community would be screened, and then accepted or rejected according to the opinion of the relevant officials. But what should a country infer if an application by a national firm is rejected? Would it know which of its own policy measures was thought to be offensive by the EC? Automatic screening of all applications would unnecessarily impede business transactions, especially when a foreign company would be bidding for a European company. Trade penalties should not be imposed on both the innocent and the guilty.

Finally, the pursuit of any kind of reciprocity has a potential cost. Other countries may retaliate. Groups of countries, therefore, may be tempted to form bilateral trading arrangements. Such arrangements covering particular service sectors have already been concluded between the US and Canada, Australia and New Zealand, the EC and Switzerland. There are also other bilateral undertakings, such as those between the UK and the US (banking, architecture) and the UK and the Netherlands (civil aviation).

Bilateral arrangements will become even more attractive should the Uruguay round fail to produce a multilateral framework for services. The disagreements that surfaced during the mid-term review session in Montreal do not augur well for a successful outcome of the round. What is at stake in the Uruguay round is not that protectionism will persist, but that there may be a proliferation of trading-blocs actively competing and discriminating against each other.

The power of the market

Individual countries may have been willing to liberalize trade as a result of the rise of conservative ideology, but on several occasions they could not afford to do otherwise. The market has forced them to remove trade barriers which have become either too costly for their domestic industry or too ineffective. For example, after the deregulation of American financial markets in the 1970s and 1980s, London could not maintain its international leadership without shedding its own restrictive practices. Member countries of the Council of Europe agreed in November 1988 to allow cross-border broadcasting under a set of common rules. They had to agree on some rules because they could not prevent reception of programmes transmitted from other countries. Technological advancement contributes to the obsolescence of regulations on foreign services which can be easily procured by domestic clients.

The establishment of international networks between service-providers and domestic clients creates vested interests which resist the imposition of restrictive trade measures. It is significant that the EC intends to apply reciprocity criteria only to new foreign companies seeking establishment within the Community. An attempt to do the same with already established foreign companies would have aroused too much opposition from those member countries that would lose a source of employment.

Technology makes trade of services across borders increasingly easier, and politics makes it difficult for governments to expel service-providers after they have established commercial presence in domestic markets. Of course, nothing can prevent a determined government from disrupting trade links. But it is hard for democratic governments to reverse the process of opening up economies to foreign services. Liberalization may be slow and may suffer setbacks. Governments may even attempt to form competing preferential trading-blocs. The question is not whether they will do it; the question is how long they can hold out against the inexorable advance of technology, the entrepreneurial ingenuity of their firms and the growing sophistication of their consumers.

Conclusion
The process of negotiating a liberal regime in services is a complex and tortuous one. It may be slowed down by a shift towards more interventionist economic policies in the major trading countries or by the pursuit of intricate reciprocal arrangements and preferential trading agreements. Indeed, this paper is primarily a warning of the complexity of the task of liberalizing services, and of all the things that can go wrong.

But the process of liberalization cannot be stopped. We may not in the near future see Koreans repairing our roads, but we will probably receive more foreign television programmes, have more of our products assembled abroad, more ships and aircraft serviced abroad, and we may even have our made-to-measure suits tailored abroad. Governments could insist on preserving legislation that makes it illegal for us to purchase foreign car insurance, or legal and medical services. Such restrictions are costly, inefficient and ultimately unenforceable. They simply provide incentives to the market to find ways around them. Through the Uruguay round of GATT negotiations and the 1992 process in Europe, governments have created for themselves the opportunity to put in place an international framework that will nourish and channel the growth of service industries and employment worldwide. The next four years are thus critical. Although one may take a sanguine view on the long-term superiority of the market, it is still essential that governments recognize the benefits of efficient policies so that valuable resources are not wasted.

REFERENCES

Balasubramanyam, V.N. (1988a). 'Interests of Developing Countries in the Liberalisation of Trade in Services', paper presented to a conference on protectionism and the Uruguay Round negotiations, Commonwealth Secretariat, London.

Balasubramanyam, V.N. (1988b). 'International Trade in Services: The Issue of Market Presence and Right of Establishment', paper presented to a conference on the GATT Uruguay Round, University of Sussex.

Baltensperger, F., and J. Dermine (1987). 'Banking Deregulation in Europe', *Economic Policy,* vol. 4, pp. 63–110.

Baumol, W. (1985). 'Productivity Policy and the Service Sector, in R. Inman (ed.), *Managing the Service Economy*, Cambridge University Press, Cambridge.

Bhagwati, J. (1984). 'Splintering and Disembodiment of Services and Developing Nations', *The World Economy*, vol. 7, no. 2, pp. 133–44.

Bhagwati, J. (1987). 'Trade in Services and the Multilateral Trade Negotiations', *The World Bank Economic Review*, vol. 1, no. 2, pp. 549–69.

Bhagwati, J. (1988). *Protectionism*, MIT Press, Cambridge, MA.

Blades, D. (1982). 'The Hidden Economy and National Accounts', *Occasional Studies*, OECD, Paris.

Blades, D. (1986). 'Goods and Services in OECD Countries', *OECD Economic Studies*, OECD, Paris.

Browning, H., and J. Singelmann (1975), *The Emergence of a Service Society*, National Technical Information Service, Springfield, VA.

Gershuny, J., and I. Miles (1983). *The New Service Economy*, Frances Pinter, London.

Giarini, O. (1987). *The Emerging Service Economy*, Pergamon Press, Oxford.

116

Gershuny, J., and I. Miles (1983). *The New Service Economy*, Frances Pinter, London.

Giarini, O. (1987). *The Emerging Service Economy*, Pergamon Press, Oxford.

Goodhart, C. (1987). 'Comment on Banking Deregulation in Europe', *Economic Policy*, vol. 4, pp. 95–8.

Goodhart, C. (1988a). 'The Costs of Regulation', in A. Seldon (ed.), *Financial Regulation or Over-Regulation?*, Institute of Economic Affairs, London.

Goodhart, C. (1988b). 'The Regulatory Debate in London', mimeo, London School of Economics, London.

Grubel, H. (1987). 'Traded Services are Embodied in Materials or People', *The World Economy*, vol. 10, no. 3, pp. 319–30.

Helleiner, G. (1987). 'Trade in Services and the Developing Countries', paper presented to a North South Roundtable on Trade, Geneva.

Hill, T.P. (1977). 'On Goods and Services', *The Review of Income and Wealth*, vol. 23, no. 4, pp. 315–38.

Hindley, B. (1986a). 'Introducing Services into GATT', mimeo, Trade Policy Research Centre, London.

Hindley, B. (1986b). 'Liberalisation of Service Transactions', mimeo, London School of Economics, London.

Hindley, B. (1987). 'Trade in Services within the European Community' in H. Giersch (ed.), *Free Trade in the World Economy*, J.C.B. Mohr, Tübingen.

Hindley, B. (1988a). 'Service Sector Protection: Considerations for Developing Countries', *World Bank Economic Review*, vol. 2, no. 2, pp. 205–23.

Hindley, B. (1988b). 'Integrated World Markets in Services: Problems and Prospects', mimeo, London School of Economics, London.

Hindley, B., and A. Smith (1984). 'Comparative Advantage and Trade in Services', *The World Economy*, vol. 7, no. 4, pp. 369–89.

Hudec, R. (1988). *Developing Countries under the GATT Legal System*, Gower for the Trade Policy Research Centre, London.

Inman, R. (1985). *Managing the Service Economy*, Cambridge University Press, Cambridge.

Jackson, J. (1988). 'Constructing a Constitution for Trade in Services', *The World Economy*, vol. 11, no. 2, pp. 187–202.

Kakabadse, M. (1987). *International Trade in Services*, Atlantic Paper No. 64, Atlantic Institute for International Affairs, Paris.

Kay, J. (1987). 'Comment on Banking Deregulation in Europe', *Economic Policy*, vol. 4, pp. 98–101.

Kay, J. (1988). 'The Forms of Regulation', in A. Seldon (ed.), *Financial Regulation or Over-Regulation?*, Institute of Economic Affairs, London.

117

References

Langhammer, R., and A. Sapir (1987). *The Economic Impact of Generalised Tariff Preferences*, Gower for the Trade Policy Research Centre, London.

Micossi, S. (1988). 'The Single European Market: Finance', *Banca Nazionale del Lavoro Quarterly Review*, June, pp. 217–35.

Monti, M. (1987). 'Integration of Financial Markets in Europe', in H. Giersch (ed.), *Free Trade in the World Economy*, J.C.B. Mohr, Tübingen.

Nicolaides, P. (1988). 'The Generalised System of Preferences and GATT', *The World Today*, vol. 44, no. 3, pp. 50–4.

Nicolaides, P. (forthcoming 1989). 'The Problem of Regulation in Traded Services', *Aussenwirtschaft*.

North-South Roundtable (1987). *Trade in Services*, Islamabad.

Ochel, W., and M. Wegner (1987). *Service Economies in Europe*, Pinter Publisher for the Commission of the European Communities, London.

Padoa-Schioppa, T. (ed.) (1987). *Efficiency, Stability and Equity*, Oxford University Press, Oxford.

Pelkmans, J., and A. Winters (1988). *Europe's Domestic Market*, Chatham House Paper No. 43, Routledge for the Royal Institute of International Affairs, London.

Petersmann, E.U. (1988). 'Functioning of the GATT System: A Constitutional Analysis', paper presented to a conference on the GATT Uruguay Round, University of Sussex.

Peterson, J., and R. Barras (1987). 'Measuring International Competitiveness in Services', *Service Industries Journal*, vol. 7, no. 2, pp. 131–42.

Petit, P. (1986). *Slow Growth and the Service Economy*, St. Martin's Press, New York.

Pryke, R. (1987). *Competition among International Airlines*, Gower for the Trade Policy Research Centre, London.

Riddle, D. (1986). *Service-Led Growth: The Role of the Service Sector in World Development*, Praeger, New York.

Riedel, J. (1987). *Myths and Reality of External Constraints on Development*, Gower for the Trade Policy Research Centre, London.

Sampson, G., and R. Snape (1985). 'Identifying the Issues in Trade in Services', *The World Economy*, vol. 8, no. 2, pp. 171–81.

Sapir, A., and E. Lutz (1980). 'Trade in Non-Factor Services: Past Trends and Current Issues', World Bank Staff Working Paper No. 410, Washington, DC.

Sapir, A., and E. Lutz (1981). 'Trade in Services: Economic Determinants and Development Related Issues', World Bank Staff Working Paper No. 480. Washington, DC.

Sharp, M. (1988). 'Inward Investment and Industrial Competitiveness', *Intereconomics*, vol. 23, pp. 241–50.

Singelmann, J. (1978). *From Agriculture to Services: The Transformation of Industrial Employment*, Sage Publications, London.

Smith, A. (1972), 'The Measurement and Interpretation of Service Output Changes', mimeo, National Economic Development Office, London.

Stalson, A. (1985). *US Service Exports and Foreign Barriers*, National Planning Association, Washington, DC.

Stanback, T. (1979). *Understanding the Service Economy*, Johns Hopkins University Press, London.

Stanback, T. et al. (1981). *Services: The New Economy*, Allanheld and Osmun, Totowa, NY.

Stigler, G. (1971). 'The Theory of Economic Regulation', *Bell Journal of Economics*, vol. 2, no. 1, pp. 3-21.

Tucker, K., and M. Sundberg (1986). *Comparative Advantage and Service Intensity in Traded Goods*, ASEAN-Australia Joint Research Project, Canberra.

Veljanovski, C. (1987). *Selling the State: Privatisation in Britain*, Weidenfeld and Nicolson, London.

Viravan, A. et al. (1987). *Trade Routes to Sustained Economic Growth*, Macmillan Press, London.

Recent related titles

Europe's Domestic Market
Jacques Pelkmans and L. Alan Winters

It was always a key aim of the European Community to achieve a common market, but the task has not yet been completed. The EC is now committed to unifying Europe's domestic market by 1992. This paper provides a critical analysis of this objective. It discusses the kind of common market which might be achieved and the economic benefits which might follow. But the authors also explore how far other economic measures need to be undertaken, and the other conditions which may need to be satisfied, if governments, industries and public opinion are to endorse the steps necessary to make the European economy more dynamic. Lastly, some comments are proffered on the potential effects of a unified market on the British economy.

Managing Exchange Rates
Peter B. Kenen

Widespread dissatisfaction with floating exchange rates has inspired new efforts to manage exchange rates among the key currencies, as well as proposals for the use of target zones and the adaptation of arrangements used in the European Monetary System. This paper examines the rationale for exchange-rate management, compares methods of management, and explores their implications for reserve and credit arrangements, the functioning of the IMF, the conduct of monetary and fiscal policies in the major countries – especially the United States – and the international coordination of macroeconomic policies. The author argues that there is a compelling case for exchange-rate management but warns against reliance on halfway measures, which are corrosive of credibility. If governments are not prepared to accept the consequences of floating rates, they must move decisively to tightly managed rates. This will require, in turn, substantial changes in reserve arrangements affecting the global role of the dollar and will also require more extensive policy coordination.

Rich Man's Farming: The Crisis in Agriculture
Michael Franklin

Excessive budgetary costs, huge surpluses and damaging trade conflicts have led world leaders to call for major changes in agricultural support. Agriculture will be prominent in the current GATT round. There seems to be a chronic tendency to overproduce and a reluctance on the part of governments to take the necessary corrective action. This study examines why a crisis situation has been allowed to develop, and proposes the most effective ways – both nationally and internationally – to achieve more rational agricultural support and trade policies. It concentrates on the current efforts to reform the Common Agricultural Policy of the European Community, on US support policies, and on the GATT negotiations.

ROUTLEDGE

www.ingramcontent.com/pod-product-compliance
Ingram Content Group UK Ltd.
Pitfield, Milton Keynes, MK11 3LW, UK
UKHW041839280225
455677UK00010B/253